THE

# SPIRIT
# WHISPERER

THE

# SPIRIT
# WHISPERER

## CHRONICLES OF A MEDIUM

CANCELLED

## JOHN HOLLAND

### HAY HOUSE

Australia • Canada • Hong Kong • India
South Africa • United Kingdom • United States

**First published and distributed in the United Kingdom by:**
Hay House UK Ltd, 292B Kensal Rd, London W10 5BE. Tel.: (44) 20 8962 1230;
Fax: (44) 20 8962 1239. www.hayhouse.co.uk

**Published and distributed in the United States of America by:**
Hay House, Inc., PO Box 5100, Carlsbad, CA 92018-5100. Tel.: (1) 760 431 7695 or
(800) 654 5126; Fax: (1) 760 431 6948 or (800) 650 5115. www.hayhouse.com

**Published and distributed in Australia by:**
Hay House Australia Ltd, 18/36 Ralph St, Alexandria NSW 2015.
Tel.: (61) 2 9669 4299; Fax: (61) 2 9669 4144. www.hayhouse.com.au

**Published and distributed in the Republic of South Africa by:**
Hay House SA (Pty), Ltd, PO Box 990, Witkoppen 2068.
Tel./Fax: (27) 11 467 8904. www.hayhouse.co.za

**Published and distributed in India by:**
Hay House Publishers India, Muskaan Complex, Plot No.3, B-2, Vasant Kunj,
New Delhi – 110 070. Tel.: (91) 11 4176 1620; Fax: (91) 11 4176 1630.
www.hayhouse.co.in

**Distributed in Canada by:**
Raincoast, 9050 Shaughnessy St, Vancouver, BC V6P 6E5. Tel.: (1) 604 323 7100;
Fax: (1) 604 323 2600

Copyright © 2010 by John Holland

The moral rights of the author have been asserted.

*Design:* Nick C. Welch • *John Holland's editor:* Simon Steel

A catalogue record for this book is available from the British Library.

ISBN 978-1-84850-950-4

Printed and bound in Great Britain by TJ International, Padstow, Cornwall.

*To Simon*

*Thank you for showing me a world I never thought
possible — and for teaching me how to
believe in myself more than I ever
could have imagined.*

*Until people are willing to
really listen — then and only then
will they truly hear the whispering of the soul.*

**— John Holland**

✦❈✦

# CONTENTS

# INTRODUCTION

There are certain important choices in your life that will determine who you are and, more important, who you will become. It is said that *everything happens for a reason,* and for the most part, I truly believe in this statement. It has proven to be true over and over in my lifetime already! When an event happens in your life, just remember it's *always* your decision what you do about it. That's the free will we all have.

Some years ago, I had a near-fatal automobile accident, which was to totally change my life. I consciously chose to let that potentially tragic event alter my course, even though I didn't fully know at the time the deeper reason for it, nor could I have possibly known the extent of the ripple effect of that one event on the thousands of lives that would be touched over the years to come. I knew that this was the big "wake-up call" that I couldn't ignore or pretend wasn't happening. After all, it was an opportunity to take a hard look at my lifestyle and to set about making some very needed changes across the board in all areas of my life. I now know that it was this event that catapulted me onto the path to becoming a *spirit whisperer.*

When you follow your path — the purpose of being all that you can be, namely a Divine being who uses all your talents, gifts, and abilities to help others — you'll start to notice doors opening in your life, offering you choices and new directions. After the accident, I made that commitment and followed a new path, which gave me the confidence to do this work. Once I made that leap of faith, new doors and meaningful opportunities appeared in all areas of my life.

As I look back while writing this book, it seems like a lifetime ago that I made that commitment to become a professional medium, as well as writing my first book, *Born Knowing*. I'm sure you won't be surprised to read that I feel like a completely different man than the John who sat down all those years ago to write the first part of my story. I never expected that what started out as a feeling inside me — that all-knowing feeling that I was different — would develop into something that would guide and influence my whole life.

My life is certainly not a typical one. I don't live a nine-to-five schedule, and I never know what's going to come up from one day to the next. There's no set script to this work, yet everything I do somehow relates back to my work. Each day, the e-mails, letters, and messages from people who've either read my books or been to one of my lectures and demonstrations or to one of my smaller group gatherings constantly touch me. I never thought that when I went to study mediumship in England back in the 1990s I'd become one of the top mediums on the circuit today. I feel blessed and honored. However, I'm forever reminding myself that I'm just an ordinary man, and I'm so grateful that I never have to work as a spirit whisperer alone, for in reality, I have the assistance of my guides, and those who have passed on.

Over the years, I've lost count of the number of books I've signed, but for me it's not so much about signing a book as about the moment I spend with that person. I still relish the intimate validations, the brief encounter, or just that all-important hug that's needed after a message has touched someone's heart and soul. It has been more than seven years since *Born Knowing* was published, and although books of a more instructional nature followed, at almost every event I'm continually asked, "John, when are you going to write another book about yourself and your experiences?"

I knew that there were so many more accounts that I hadn't been able to include in my first book, not to mention all the new experiences and teachings — both personally and professionally — that have taken place since then. I always knew that when the time was right, they would be told.

Over these years, I've been blessed with a fantastic lineup of wonderful guests on my weekly radio show *Spirit Connections*. If someone had told me ten years ago that I'd be hosting my own radio show, well, you can imagine what my response would have been at the time — something along the lines of "Get real . . . what do I know about hosting a radio show?!" It has now been more than four years since I began my weekly program, and I look forward to each and every show as I reach people all around the world. I've traveled to almost every part of the United States, the UK, and Australia giving lectures, demonstrations, and workshops — and working with some of the top names in the industry. I may be a teacher, but at the same time, I'll always be first and foremost a student.

I feel deeply honored to be part of this spiritual awakening that so many of you have come to realize is a major part of your life. I hope that for those of you who've never read a spiritual book before, who've never meditated or considered what happens to the physical body after death, this book will be the catalyst for change. I often say in my lectures, especially to the new people or the skeptics, "If you leave here wondering how I could have said something that I couldn't possibly have known; or if you were moved by a message given from the Spirit World; and if maybe I opened a door you thought you would never walk through; and if you go on and do your own investigation or study of the continuity of life, the power of your own spirit, and your soul — then I feel I've done my job."

### Why *The Spirit Whisperer?*

The title of this book came to me one day when I was writing, as I'd been sitting there for a long time pondering a suitable title. I wanted to find one that would somehow encapsulate the next chapter of my life story. Almost out of the blue, it came to me. In a flash, or what I call inspiration, there was the title. In reality this is *exactly* what happens to me, as a spirit whisperer, when I link with the Other-Side. Thoughts, words, images, and feelings are whispered and imprinted on my own soul and consciousness so that I can give back everything to the person who's receiving the message.

This is *not* a book about death. It's actually a book about the living, both in this world and the next. There is no death. As a medium, I consider death to be a profound experience, somewhat of a birth, a soul passing from one realm to another. Some people regard it as a miraculous experience and welcome it with wonder and respect. There are those who view it with fear and regret for things not said or done. I feel leaving this world with regret is the hardest thing for any person. The same goes for those who are left behind. That's why I advise people to say and do what they have to with those who are in their lives now.

I know that some of you who are reading this book are going through a process of bereavement. When you lose someone, bereavement is an important and natural part of accepting and coming to terms with the loss. It can be a powerful, healthy, and healing process in its own right, which will help you to let go of some of the pain. Sometimes people feel that if they stop grieving, then they're somehow saying good-bye to that person forever and will forget them. Bereavement is a process that you should move through rather than hold on to. I hope that this book offers some comfort for you, as well as healing and possibly some closure.

I totally respect that not everyone will share all my views. When I write, I do so from my own perspective, and I want everyone to know that these are *my* own experiences. It is my hope that you can learn or be inspired by them.

This book chronicles the past seven years of my life and includes some enlightening and heartfelt real-life case studies, and also takes you a step further back in time to when I was a student and some of the extraordinary things that I've witnessed and experienced. If I hadn't experienced them myself or seen them with my own eyes, I might find them hard to understand or accept.

Throughout the book, I've provided some real insights into what it's like to work as a spirit whisperer and the unusual and unique world of mediumship. I have intentionally used a few stories from my previous books to jog your memory. Some of them are so moving, and have such strong messages, that I feel they are worth repeating. However, if you're new to my work, then I hope that this book will help you understand where I'm coming from and that you can gain a better understanding of mediumship and Spiritualism as a whole.

I hope that you'll enjoy some of the candid stories of readings I've given to clients, including those who've had their own After Death Communications (ADCs) — from the outrageous to the profound. I also hope it will help you begin to notice your own special communications from your loved ones. Throughout this book, I'll explain some of the signs and symbols that loved ones use when they try to communicate. You'll hear me repeat one of my favorite sayings that many of you may have heard me say onstage: "Those on the Other-Side want to talk to you — as much as you want to talk to them!"

I will also divulge for the first time some of the extraordinary para-normal occurrences I've witnessed throughout my career and provide a rare glimpse behind the scenes of what it's like to be a "psychic time machine" for one of the TV shows I was featured in.

I also describe the time I had an amazing session with psy-chiatrist and past-life expert Brian Weiss, M.D., the author of the best-selling book *Many Lives, Many Masters,* when he regressed me — an experience that I hope you'll enjoy reading about. For me, it was enlightening, and confirmed that the journey of the soul never ends, but constantly moves forward and evolves.

As a medium, I find that the time when my work strikes home most is when I read for parents who've lost a child. Without a doubt, these are some of the most touching, heartfelt stories; and it's my hope that when you read that chapter, you may find comfort and healing from the knowledge that your child does still live on. I've also written a whole chapter on sensitive and psychic children, as I'm dedicated to helping parents and teachers who have a psy-chic child themselves.

Since I am also a lover of all animals, I had to include a chapter on them, too. For some of us, our animals are our children and are our spiritual companions, because they teach us so much about ourselves as they give us continual unconditional love.

Anyone who knows me, the real me, will tell you that I'm a highly sensitive man. After all, how could I do this work if I weren't? It's like a double-edged sword, since when I'm sitting opposite two parents who've lost a beautiful little girl, I've got to be superhuman not to feel the depth of their sadness, their loss, their emotion. As a result, there's been many a reading where I've shared their tears.

I've tried to figure out what this work will eventually do to me. Someone once asked me, "John, what does the future hold for you?" Such a loaded question, and in a way, I've stopped trying to answer it. I know that with my time here, I have to give my life in service for those in the Spirit World. I really feel I chose to do this work and have done it many times in previous lives.

I'm content to devote my life to the work, knowing that in those precious few minutes when the link is created, I can act as that conduit for messages of love, forgiveness, hope, joy, healing, and in many cases, closure, to put peace of mind to something that was left unanswered. As I've said, it's certainly not your typical job; it's not something that you can start at nine and finish at five, Monday to Friday. If I'd wanted to become a doctor, a lawyer, or a designer, then I would have done so. Nevertheless, this is my life, dedicated to the service of helping others.

You can read this book in order, cover to cover, or you can read it by choosing any chapter you feel drawn to. I also occasionally repeat small bits of background information to help those who choose to read different chapters at different times. I hope that *The Spirit Whisperer* will be an inspiring book you'll want to read over and over, as many of the stories will touch your heart as well as your soul, as you discover that love is eternal and will never die. Remember that we are and always will be connected to each other here, as well as to those who have gone on before us.

# CHAPTER 1

# THE RISE OF MEDIUMSHIP

"How many of you are the *different* ones in your family?" That's the question that I ask of all my audiences at every lecture and demonstration. More than 80 percent of any audience is likely to raise their hands as they nod their heads in acknowledgment. But what do I mean by different? Let me try to explain. If you're the sort of person who questions whether there's more to life than what is directly in front of you, then you're a little different from the rest of society. If you've had your own spiritual experiences, are somehow drawn to metaphysics and New Age, and have a keen interest in psychic phenomena; or if you know your soul is trying to reach out to you to follow its guidance, then again you're a little different.

I was always the different one in my family. I was extrasensitive and knew things as a child that I couldn't possibly have known or guessed. I'd know who was about to unexpectedly visit or which relative was ill. I'd often know what people were about to say just before they opened their mouths. I'd see spirit people in my bedroom and always wondered whether I was dreaming. Yet none of this fazed me at the time, for those experiences had been there since I was born. How could I be afraid of what has always been a part of me and my life? So let me ask the question again: Are we really different or are we simply just awake? If you're reading this book, then you probably know there's more to this life and are tired of sleepwalking through it.

I'm sure that many people who come to my lectures do so out of curiosity. They may be unfamiliar with what mediumship is all about and exactly how I can help them. One of the questions I'm often asked is: "Exactly what is a medium?" Throughout the ages, there have been numerous definitions. Typically, a medium acts as a connection or a conduit between this physical world and that of the Spirit. I simply tell people to imagine me as the "middleman." As a medium, I've had my fair share of being criticized, tested, idolized, and *yes* . . . even laughed at. All this doesn't bother me as it did in the past. I have a job to do, and I will continue to assist and to help validate that we are all in fact eternal beings with unlimited potential.

No matter how you look at it, we have an enthusiastic and eager willingness to embrace the possibility of life after death. Since man first began to walk the earth, he has constantly strived to understand the nature of his own existence. I feel it's an ongoing desire that resonates deep inside our hearts and souls. I almost defy anyone to say he hasn't wondered about this at some point in his life and asked himself the question: *Do we really continue to live on after death?*

According to the science of physics, *nothing* is lost in the universe. We are eternal and have always existed as Spirit. We existed before we were born and will continue to exist long after our physical bodies die. So with that said, then it's true, "You cannot die for the life of you!" The *real* you will continue to live on after you leave this physical world, and I believe that it's my job as a spirit whisperer to help validate just that.

### The Spirit World Breaks Through

In my first book, I wrote an incredible story of how those on the Other-Side showed up for the first time in one of my psychic readings. It was a day I'll truly never forget! It seems like a lifetime ago that I began to do this work. I don't feel that I'm the same man who wrote *Born Knowing!* After all, so much has changed, and I've learned, grown, and developed beyond all my early expectations; I just simply had to get out of my own way.

I'm going back to the beginning here, more than 17 years ago. I was working as a psychic and *not* a medium in those days. Little did I realize that those on the Other-Side had their own plans for how I was going to work in the future. There's quite a big difference between practicing as a psychic and as a medium. There's a wonderful saying that goes: "All mediums are psychic, but not all psychics are mediums." Let me explain that more fully. A psychic reads your aura (your past, present, and potential future), whereas a medium gets information directly from those on the Other-Side.

It was while living in Los Angeles in the 1990s that I was involved in a serious automobile accident. To this day, I'm convinced, as I said previously, that it was this very accident that put me on the path that I now walk. Sometimes it *does* take a drastic life change to truly begin living! After the accident, the psychic abilities I'd experienced as a child, the same ones I'd pushed away at a very young age, were now back, but this time they were a hundred times stronger. When my abilities started to surface, many of my friends were encouraging me to give readings. All my old demons started to tug away inside. I hesitated and fought a running battle with myself rather than making the choice to just do it! Even though I knew I was being guided, I didn't want to be called names again or be pointed at. I didn't want to have to deal with skeptics, and what most people don't realize is that the responsibility of this work can be overwhelming at times. After all, others' lives are at stake.

Finally, after a lot more study on psychic phenomena and understanding how my own abilities worked and functioned, I was more confident to move forward on a journey that I knew I had to take. The continued support of my friends helped enormously, so I made the decision to start reading for people, but only as a psychic.

Slowly people began to hear about me, and an artist named Maury, who'd heard about me from a friend, came to see me for a reading. She wanted to discuss certain areas of her life, and as she sat down, she explained that she'd been feeling as if there were a number of different roads springing up in front of her. She asked me if I could give her some guidance on the direction that was for her highest good. I don't really recall the exact moment that things started to happen, but one minute we were talking about her design career, and the next I felt as if something had shifted in the room — and it had. These days with all my years of experience, I refer to this shift as "the quickening." It's hard to explain what happened in simple terms, but it felt a bit like everything was just going a little faster, as though someone had turned up the switch. More significantly, it meant that Maury and I weren't alone anymore . . . not by a long shot.

As I looked at Maury again, I suddenly noticed that sitting right beside her was an elderly woman with an incredibly warm smile. I saw her there as clear as day. I felt the uncontrollable urge to tell my client immediately, but I didn't really know the best way to say it. So I just blurted it out: "Maury, there's an older woman sitting beside you, and there's something strange about her clothes — nothing matches. Oh! And yes, she keeps talking about a diamond." Maury let out a scream, I screamed, she hugged me, and I hugged her!

I calmed down a bit, reminding myself to take a moment to breathe. I could clearly hear this old woman's voice in my head. She was relentless, saying the same thing over and over again: "She'll know who I am. Mention the diamond! Mention the diamond!" This was all so new to me. I'd never done a reading like this before. Of course, as you'd expect, I did exactly as she asked. I just pushed on, and found myself talking so fast that I didn't even stop to check in with Maury to see how she was reacting to this tidal wave of messages. I didn't have to wait long, though, because all of a sudden she let out a loud gasp for air and just burst into tears. It took me by surprise, and I got up to console her, asking, "So, who *is* this woman?"

In a broken voice, she said, "John, it's my Great-aunt Ada, who raised me. She was color blind, yet she insisted on choosing her own clothes. Our family never knew what she'd show up wearing, and this diamond ring I'm wearing right now was hers, and she left it to me!" She held out her hand so I could admire the ring that was catching the light in the room perfectly.

Maury continued to tell me how she and Ada had a very strong bond, right up to her death ten years earlier. "She loved me and was always so kind to me. I could always count on her. Even though she's gone, I have something to remind me of her. I inherited her diamond ring." Maury sobbed. "I miss her so much."

I sat there slightly amazed myself, not quite comprehending what had just happened. Was this how it was going to be for the rest of my life? Was this my destiny?

As my client composed herself, we sat down again, and I suggested that we continue our journey together.

"Is she still there?" Maury whispered.

"Yes, she's here," I said. "She's smiling, and she's asking me to tell you that she's always close by." Half an hour later, Maury hugged me once again on the doorstep and left with a huge smile on her face.

I collapsed on the couch. I couldn't believe what had happened. I lay there and said to myself, *Great. First, I have to accept that I'm a psychic with all that goes with that responsibility. Now I'm talking to the dead!*

At the time, I had a sneaking suspicion why this was a turning point, and why all of a sudden I was communicating with spirits who'd departed this physical world. For about two years, I'd been giving psychic readings and in some way, I must have reached an entirely new level of ability. Not only was I *seeing* these spirits, but they were also *communicating* directly with me, or should I say *through* me.

Something equally odd happened with that early reading, which I really want to share. I found out later that Maury couldn't wait to play the cassette tape of our session. She told me weeks later that when I was talking about her design career, my voice sounded perfectly normal on the tape. However, when Great-aunt Ada appeared to "do her thing," the tape just sped up all on its own, to the point where everything sounded like it was on hyperspeed.

When Ada's energy faded and she was gone, the tape returned to normal, and Maury was able to hear our voices again. Somehow, the Spirit World was jump-starting the entire atmosphere.

This marked the first time that *they* were present during a reading. From that point on, they showed up almost every time and started to make their presence known beforehand. It was certainly not that unusual to be driving to a reading or lecture, only to find the backseat crowded with spirits jostling for position to be the first one to speak.

As always, I wasn't ready to accept this without understanding what was going on, and I needed to put some logic around it, if that was possible. I wanted to know why this was happening, and better yet, what I should do about it. There was no time to delay, so I set out to do as much research as I could on the complex subject of mediumship. Almost every book I read was from the UK and constantly mentioned Spiritualism. The questions swirled around inside my head. *What is Spiritualism? Is it a faith or a religion? Does science come into it? On the other hand, is it simply a philosophy? Would this faith help me understand what was happening to me?*

I knew that I had to find answers to the questions that were plaguing me. As a student, I knew that I wouldn't rest until I'd gained as much knowledge as possible. I was a man with a mission.

### The Emergence of Spiritualism

Spiritualism is a belief system that has its foundations in the continuity of life and communication with Spirit through the spiritual ability of mediumship. For many, it's also a religion, a philosophy, and . . . a way of life. The Spiritualists' faith has a very calming and healing effect, as it is their belief that we don't die and that our loved ones who have passed on are still very much alive and well in Spirit. Sadly, too many Hollywood movies have portrayed this faith in a somewhat spooky light, giving the wrong impression about what Spiritualism is today.

Spiritualism was actually founded in 1848 in America when

two teenage sisters were experiencing strange happenings in their small cottage home in Hydesville, New York. Disturbing noises, knockings and raps, movements of objects, and other supernatural phenomena were occurring day after day.

The Fox sisters, Margeretta and Kate, would often hear very loud bangs and raps coming from the walls, which kept them awake. The noises didn't seem to emanate from any one specific point, so they decided to come up with their own form of communication to see if the noises would respond back to them. The sisters began to clap their hands, and in return, the raps mimicked the same number of claps. They were highly perplexed, wondering if the noises and raps had some kind of intelligence.

At one point, the sisters yelled out, "Knock twice for yes and once for no!" To their absolute amazement, they discovered that the raps were answering them! In earnest, they decided to devise another code so that they could communicate further. They had the idea of using raps to spell out the letters in the alphabet. One rap for the letter *a*, two raps for the letter *b*, three for the letter *c*, and so on. They were very excited because they could actually have a conversation with whatever or whoever was making the noise. They patiently wrote out the whole alphabet letter by letter in their new rapping-type language.

Through this form of communication, they discovered that the noises were actually coming from the spirit of a man named Charles B. Rosna. He was a traveling salesman who'd once lived in the sisters' house with another family with the last name of Bell. The Fox family moved in a few years later.

Through a series of raps, Charles told the sisters that he had been murdered, and that all his valuables had been stolen. To the sisters' complete surprise, he told them that he was buried in the basement! Using their newfound special code, he also told them about a tin box that had been buried with him.

Soon the sisters' mom got involved in what they were doing, and she came up with a great idea. She wondered if this spirit of Charles Rosna could not only hear her family, but could actually *see* them as well. Mrs. Fox tried a little experiment. She would clap her hands a number of times silently and then ask the spirit to bang out how many times she silently clapped. To their surprise, the number of raps came back exactly the same. They all stood there in total amazement, wondering what to do next.

The news of the sisters spread like wildfire. People came from all over to experience the phenomena for themselves. People were amazed by how *normal* the Fox sisters appeared. They were just two simple young girls who had a basic education and were not particularly religious in any way. From what everyone could see and experience, these girls were, in fact, communicating with the spirit of a man who had died tragically some years before in that very house.

Of course, the story doesn't end there. Sure enough, the basement floor was excavated, and the remains of one Mr. Charles B. Rosna, the traveling salesman, were found. Moreover, just as he'd told the sisters, there was a tin box lying right beside him. The psychic happenings at the Foxes' home encouraged other people to try communicating with the Spirit World for themselves. Many individuals across the country were forming groups in an attempt to communicate with loved ones who had gone on before them. Many discovered that some people were able to communicate with spirits far more than others, and soon, mediumship was on the rise; and Spiritualism, a new religion of faith, had begun.

Over the years, the Fox sisters went on to demonstrate their mediumship and talk about their experiences. They helped others by using their unique form of mediumship in further attempts to communicate with other spirits.

Although Spiritualism was actually founded in America, it also flourished in England. Many of its followers were women, and it was the only religion where females could speak out and be heard. Many members also supported the abolition of slavery and women's suffrage.

There are still Spiritualist churches in the United States, but not nearly as many as there are "across the pond," as they say. Mediumship not only caught the attention of the British people, but royalty and even wise scholars like Sir Arthur Conan Doyle developed an interest in the subject. To this day, many continue their quest to learn as much as they can about this fascinating topic.

# CHAPTER 2

## PRINCIPLES OF SPIRITUALISM

Most religions have some belief in the afterlife — some more than others. I firmly believe that it's important to follow some kind of faith, for each offers its own guidance. In the case of Spiritualism, it has its own teachings, which can assist us when it's our time to cross over. Although I value what Spiritualism teaches, I try to encompass and honor many belief systems, from Catholicism and Buddhism to Kabbalah and more. I feel that each serves its own unique purpose in providing tools and teachings for our spiritual journey. I like to use the analogy of the spokes of a wheel, in that each spoke represents a different religion or faith. Although each is independent of the other, every spoke in the wheel is going to the same place.

We're all born with the spark from the Divine (our spirit), so when our spirit finally crosses over, that spark will leave the physical "jacket" it's encased in, and slip back into the Spirit World where we originated. We all survive death no matter what (if any) religion we choose to believe.

When I began my own journey many years ago, I was attracted to the principles of Spiritualism and how these beliefs bond us together as spiritual beings. There are seven principles in total, and if we could all live by them, what an amazing world it would be!

Through philosophy and practical demonstrations, Spiritualism aims to provide evidence that a part of everyone (the spirit) continues to exist after death and for eternity. Spiritualism does not tie its followers to a creed or dogma, but the philosophy is based on the seven principles that were written in the 19th century through the mediumship of Emma Hardinge Britten. They are widely accepted by Spiritualist organizations around the world.

The following is an interpretation of these principles from the SNU (Spiritualists National Union), who have kindly given permission to use these definitions. (I have made minimal changes for clarity throughout.)

## THE FIRST PRINCIPLE —
## THE FATHERHOOD OF GOD

By the study of Nature — that is, by trying to understand the Laws of Cause and Effect, which govern all that is happening around us — we recognize that there is a creative force in the universe. This force, or energy, not only created the whole universe, but also life itself in its many forms and is continuing to create today. The effects of this eternal creation can be seen all around us, and this leads us to the evidence that "God" — "The Creative Force" — manifests directly, or indirectly, in all things. We know this power as God and as we are part of the Life created by God, we acknowledge God as our Father.

## THE SECOND PRINCIPLE —
## THE BROTHERHOOD OF MAN

Because we all come from the same universal life source, in effect we're one large family, small individual off-shoots, which come from the whole. This means that all mankind is part of a brotherhood. A brotherhood is a community for mutual support and comfort. We are all members of the same Divine family. We need to share our joys as well as our burdens; we need to understand the needs of other individuals in order to assist them as part of our service to each other. As we learn to give, so must we also learn to receive, thereby achieving the necessary balance for our life. We must look not only to the material necessities of our fellow creatures, but also to their spiritual needs, and help those in need to become strong and worthy of their relationship in the Family of God.

---

## THE THIRD PRINCIPLE — COMMUNION OF SPIRITS AND THE MINISTRY OF ANGELS

All religions believe in life after death, but only Spiritualism shows that it is true by demonstrating that communication with departed spirits can and does take place. Spiritualist Churches provide one of the venues where communication, through mediumship, is possible and many loved relatives and friends take advantage of this opportunity to continue to take an interest in our welfare. There are also spirit people/teachers who are dedicated to the welfare and service of mankind. Some (e.g., Silver Birch) bring inspiration and teachings, while others work within the healing ministry.

---

## THE FOURTH PRINCIPLE — CONTINUOUS EXISTENCE OF THE HUMAN SOUL

It's scientifically proven that matter (being part of the creative force, or energy) cannot be destroyed; it merely changes its form. Spirit, as part of the Creative Force is, therefore, indestructible. On the death of the physical body, the spirit continues as an integral part of a world, which interpenetrates our world but in a different dimension. This world is referred to as the Spirit World. In spirit life, we have a spirit body, which until we progress far enough, is a replica of our earthly body. We are the same individuals in every way with the same personalities and characteristics and we change only by progression, or otherwise, because of our own efforts. Our personal responsibilities do not stop at death.

## THE FIFTH PRINCIPLE — PERSONAL RESPONSIBILITY

This principle places responsibility for wrongful thoughts and deeds where it belongs, i.e., with the individual. It is the acceptance of responsibility for every aspect of our lives and the use to which we place our lives depends entirely upon ourselves. It is not possible for any other person, or outside influence, to interfere with our spiritual development, unless we are willing to allow this. No one can put right the wrongdoing except the offender. As we are given freedom of choice (free will), we're also given the ability to recognize what is right from what is wrong. We are totally, as well as personally, responsible.

## THE SIXTH PRINCIPLE — COMPENSATION AND RETRIBUTION HEREAFTER FOR ALL GOOD AND EVIL DEEDS DONE ON EARTH

As with all the other Principles, the natural laws apply and this one echoes the law of Cause and Effect (as you sow, so shall you reap). One cannot be cruel and vindictive toward others and expect love and popularity in return. It must be understood that the compensatory or retributive effects of this law operate now — on Earth — they do not wait until we begin to live in the Spirit World.

## The Seventh Principle — Eternal Progress Open to Every Human Soul

In every heart, there exists the desire for progress, and to every human spirit belongs the power to progress in wisdom and love. All who desire to tread the path that leads to perfection are able to pursue it. The rate of progress is directly proportional to the desire for mental and spiritual understanding. If we do our best in Earth life to follow our inward prompting or intuitions, we shall find progress very easy, on Earth as in spirit; if not, every step in advancement will follow a struggle against imperfections, which we ourselves will have worked into our natures. Within the Family of God, with all the advantages that our realization of that state can give us, we are all given the opportunity to be responsible for our own eternal progress.

---

These seven principles have influenced the way I've lived my life, and after I read them for the first time, I realized that I've held the same beliefs. The principles speak about honoring nature and the earth, that we're all connected to each other, that the soul is eternal; and above all, they encourage us to be responsible for our actions, teaching us about the law of cause and effect, and most important, about love.

These were written so many years ago, but as you read them, you may understand them for yourself; many other authors, lecturers, and scholars teach the same principles but in a different way or format.

Although it's wonderful to watch a legitimate medium work, I feel it's just as important to teach the philosophy of Spiritualism. I believe that each and every one of us is given the choice of free will, and what we do here as spiritual beings — having human experiences — will affect our spirits when it's our time to finally go home to the Spirit World.

## *A Place of Faith*

People who have chosen to follow the path of Spiritualism hold services in their own churches, but they're by no means exclusive, as most Spiritualist churches welcome everyone. They're wonderful places to share experiences with people from all walks of life. There are meetings, classes, and workshops on mediumship and psychic development. There are special events that usually relate to the science, philosophy, and religion of Spiritualism. The services are often uplifting; and include music, prayer, spiritual healing, a sermon, and often messages from Spirit.

I still remember with enormous affection the two years that I spent studying in the UK. I'd barely gotten off the plane before I was inquiring about Spiritualist churches. I wanted to know how many there were, where they were, and how to find out about their services. I could hardly wait. It turned out that Bristol, the city in which I lived, had ten churches to choose from — all right on my doorstep! Brilliant! Within a few days I'd wasted no time in making my way to one. It was a big moment for me, because this would be my first time in a real Spiritualist church. I thought I might be a bit nervous as I approached the entrance, but my feet didn't stop — they practically ran through those doors. I'm sure that anyone looking at me that night would have seen the excitement and anticipation written all over my face.

It was a typically gray, somewhat raw night with light drizzle, but I hardly noticed it. Two women greeted me as I walked in, and as I said hello back, they immediately noticed my accent. I braced myself, fully preparing to be told that only members were allowed in or something like that.

"Welcome, dear friend," they said. "You can sit wherever you like."

I noticed that everything from the pews to the brightly colored stained-glass windows looked like many of our churches back home. For a moment, I was overcome, awestruck that I was finally here. Only days earlier, I'd been saying my good-byes to friends in Los Angeles, and now here I was at my first Spiritualist service. I didn't really know what to expect, so I took a seat and tried hard not to look too out of place, feeling very much like the "new boy" on the block!

The service began with the president of the church speaking for a moment, and then the medium was introduced. She was a short, well-dressed, quite ordinary-looking woman who looked like someone's mom. After all, I had no idea what other mediums looked like. I hadn't met any! I quickly found out that besides linking with Spirit, it was also up to the medium to give an *inspired address,* which meant that Spirit would speak through her. I felt totally as though I'd arrived. I knew I was in the right place and settled back to watch her work. She was a consummate professional. During her opening address, words just seemed to flow; and strangely, it seemed as though she was talking directly to me. It was as if she knew what I needed to hear *at that exact moment.* I wondered if, somehow, in her own way, she knew I'd just arrived; but more important, that I was on a fast-track learning curve.

After about 20 minutes, she started her demonstration, which included connecting some of the members of the congregation with their loved ones who had passed. I imagined that if a Spiritualist received a message, he'd rush home and tell his family. I played out the scenario in my head, hearing the conversation over the supper table: "I heard from Dad this evening." And another family member would respond, "Oh, yes? How is he, and what did he say?"

As I've said previously, Spiritualists are raised to believe in the continuity of life, and mediums aren't stars to them — they're just the messengers.

From that very first night, I was hooked. I started attending church regularly over the following months, and the services became a firm fixture in my schedule. Nothing could get in their way. During the course of those first few services, the visiting mediums would often pick me out of the crowd, delivering a message from my grandfather or another relative. One of the most significant messages was when a lovely woman told me, "Young man, you have beautiful colors around you. Someday *you* will be up here doing this work." There it was again . . . encouragement to move ahead. It was as though my destiny was preordained. Nevertheless, one of my biggest life-changing experiences was to come, when a well-known medium visited the church one evening — a man who would never know how influential he would be in my life.

The evening began with this man's wonderful way of working with the congregation and commanding the platform. Then he looked directly at me, pointing with his finger as he said, "You, sir! Yes, *you!* You were born with the gift of Spirit." He certainly had a way with words, and the directness of his statement sent chills up and down my spine. I felt like a student back at school, and I'm sure I sat more upright in my chair. I felt very aware that everyone was suddenly looking at me, as all heads in the church turned to face me. For a split second, I hadn't fully taken in what he'd just said, which was when I finally realized that he was actually talking about me!

He hardly stopped to draw breath, and quickly went on, "I also have your guide here with me, and after the service I'll speak to you about him." As soon as the service ended, I could barely contain myself, but went up and sheepishly introduced myself. He shook my hand, and smiled warmly.

"I don't usually do this, but your guide is very strong, and so firmly with you. He really wants me to tell you about him," he said.

I was spellbound, and could only offer a nod to acknowledge that I was taking it all in.

"Your guide is a Tibetan monk," he continued. "He's working with you and says that you are exactly where you should be at this point in your development. His message is quite simple, it's this: 'All you need to do is let go and trust.'" At that, he stopped. He'd given me what I needed to hear.

This was my very first introduction to one of my guides, and of course, much later in my development, I would find that I actually have three of them, who were drawn by a wonderful psychic artist from England named Coral Polge. I write more about this in Chapter 5.

Over the months of preparation before I left Los Angeles to head over to the UK, I read a lot about spirit guides, but this was just the evidence I hoped to hear. I remember that as a child, I'd often dreamed of praying men with shaved heads and brightly colored robes. Now, of course, I realize that they were Tibetan monks . . . and one of them was now one of my guides. What an evening! What a revelation!

Sitting on the bus on my way home that night, I vowed to listen to my guide and do exactly as I was told. I recited those words repeatedly in my head, so they were firmly imprinted — not that I was likely to forget them. *Let go and trust.* Of course, that's always easier said than done.

Even to this day, any opportunity I get, you'll still find me in churches singing, praying, and meditating, as well as experiencing the healings that are offered. I love watching the old and young mediums lecture, and demonstrate their mediumship, as they bring comfort to those who attend.

It's true to say that Spiritualist beliefs and their churches may not resonate with everyone, but I found that the love and friendship, being with like-minded people in these churches, and the philosophy that is taught were just what I needed to continue my journey of helping others. I find it comforting that Spiritualism teaches us that God can be found in all things and that we're all connected; and since the spiritual force is in fact in all things, there will never be any discrimination. Spirit welcomes all. If we could all live with that belief, what a beautiful world it would be.

# CHAPTER 3

# INSPIRATIONAL MEDIUMSHIP

It's rare that a day goes by when some sort of random thought, idea, notion, or hunch doesn't pop into your head. For example, it may be when you're sitting in a coffee shop, or at the hair salon, or just having a soak in the bath. There's no rhyme or reason, and it doesn't matter where you are or what you're doing. Often, they come when you're not thinking about or focusing on anything in particular. Some people spend a lifetime studying the wonders and miracles of the mind, asking themselves, *Where do these thoughts come from?*

I wish I could give you a definitive answer here, something that would offer total clarity, but as with so many questions on this subject, there are numerous answers. Some people believe that these random thoughts and ideas come from the Universe, God, a guide, or just from your own soul. Of course, it can equally be explained as part of a fine-tuned intuition; or for those who wish to play devil's advocate, you could say it's simply conjured up from your own mind or imagination.

As a boy, I devoured books on magic, spirits, ghosts, religion, theology, astronomy, and science. I was hungry for knowledge. You would find me curled up with picture books that would show magnificent places and people around the world. It's said that "knowledge is power," but maybe this was part of my early training to develop my sixth sense in preparation for becoming a spirit whisperer. Little did I know that years later, and now working as an established and reputable medium, I'd have to expand my consciousness to such a high level to work effectively as a channel for those in Spirit. I've devoted my life for the past 20 years to continually training so that I can act as a conduit for the Spirit World, to establish that unique connection of subtle impressions, thoughts, ideas, and words from those on the Other-Side.

People who take part in my workshops often ask me how they can move to the next level, having taken the initial first steps of learning to awaken their psychic potential. In a way, it's a bit like becoming a world-class athlete. You don't get to the top without dedication and constant training. You literally have to train almost day after day, or in my case during those early years, it was every week! Those of you who have read my first book will recall that I spent two formative years studying in the UK. Imagine this young, naïve American moving to another country where no one knew him, arriving in the UK filled with questions that he knew he had to find answers to.

I remember this time with huge affection, as it became the foundation of everything I've learned to this day. I began my training by what is known as *sitting in circle*. A circle simply means a group of like-minded people, whether it's for meditation, psychic development, or the development of a certain type of mediumship — all sitting together and sharing each other's energy as you develop. These circles are usually led by a teacher or a medium who has had more experience and can watch and give advice as your abilities emerge and begin to unfold.

I didn't know what to expect, and for anyone thinking of taking this next step, I'd suggest you find a reputable circle with people who are inclined to guide you and explain the basics, as well as the mechanics, of mediumship. I was lucky to land on my feet with my first circle with other mediums who were developing their abilities. Some circles are *closed circles,* which is when you have to be formally invited to join, as I was in this case. In addition, there are what are known as *open circles,* where anyone can practice their psychic abilities or develop their mediumship further.

This is a wonderful practice, and I spent almost every Tuesday evening for the better part of two years sitting in that cozy room on the outskirts of Bristol. It was in one of those typically British tightly packed terraced streets, where all the front doors seemed to be painted a different color. If I was late, I'd find the door locked! This taught me to take it seriously, apart from punctuality, and only made me even more committed to develop my newfound abilities. Even at this early stage, I felt that my destiny was being mapped out, and that this was something that was about to become a huge part of my life.

Fortunately, this particular circle had a professional medium leading the group who gave us guidance. She would also observe us while we meditated and help us with our technique. She would see our guides and the spirit people as they drew close, making us aware they were there. In my case, it was just a matter of slowing down long enough to become aware. It was about learning to raise my own vibrational energy and to recognize what was happening at that incredible moment when the link was made. I was so fortunate with this circle, since not only did it show me how to blend and develop a stronger link with Spirit, to receive and give spirit messages, but it also focused on how we can receive Divine inspiration from our guides and helpers. The circle leader believed that while it's helpful and healing to hear from your loved ones on the Other-Side with specific messages of hope, it's just as beneficial to hear inspirational wisdom from your guides, who are much wiser and more experienced. She would tell us that it's often from such wisdom that true inspiration is born.

### Proving Myself

Inspiration has been channeled for thousands of years from Spirit. Communication comes through a myriad of different channels and often brings us information about birth and death, as well as the mysteries and wonders of life. During my time in England,

and without a second thought, I threw myself in, attending count-less mediumship demonstrations, many of which would start with the medium giving an inspirational lecture. I later discovered that these lectures were unrehearsed and completely spontaneous. No teleprompter, no notes, and for someone who was soaking it up for the first time, I found that the inspirational words would often resonate for many days to follow.

It's fascinating to me that when an inspirational speech or lecture is given, most people feel that the speaker, and the wisdom imparted, addressed them specifically. Few subjects were off-limits in the presentations. Time after time, I was privileged to witness the mediums offering their insights on a subject that was chosen by someone in the audience. It was amazing to sit back and listen to the words that would just miraculously flow, as though some hid-den Oscar-winning scriptwriter had been at work. Nowadays, when I give my keynote lectures, there are times when I'm completely astounded by where the words come from. While I consider myself well read and educated, I fully appreciate my own limitations, so when I'm given true inspiration, I've learned to acknowledge and respect where it's coming from. I never take it for granted, and I'm enormously grateful.

Every time I got home after one of those lectures or demonstra-tions, I would think about how I couldn't wait to put some of my newfound ideas into practice at the next circle meeting. I wrote about these evenings in *Born Knowing,* and there was one such night that I'll never forget. It was the very first time I was introduced to the circle and its members. It's such a special story for me that I want to repeat it in this book for those who haven't read it before.

The afternoon had dragged on and on. I must have looked at my watch a hundred times, staring out of the window, waiting for a blue car to pull up. Margaret, who was to be my introducer and mentor, had offered to pick me up on her way. Eventually she arrived and off we went. After ushering me into a small waiting room on the side of the entrance hall, Margaret gave me a brief explanation about what was about to happen, but more important, what was expected of me! She led me into the main room, and I was introduced to the seven other people, who sat in a perfect neat circle. They were clearly waiting for me. The whole atmosphere was electric, although fully charged with love. I sensed it immediately. I realized later that they'd just finished their group meditation as they prepared to meet me. That's one of the purposes of meditation — to fill the room with energy. I felt all their eyes staring at me. As I sat down, I tried desperately not to let any of them see my knees, which were visibly shaking. I'd never expected to feel this nervous.

One by one, the group members introduced themselves, and after what seemed like an age, it was finally my turn to say hello. I gave them a brief summary of my life as a psychic and a medium, and told them the somewhat bizarre yet synchronistic story of how I'd come to be in England. The words just flowed from me in a way I hadn't experienced before. I felt so open and free in this softly lit room with its sparse yet comfortable furnishings. All my earlier inhibitions and nerves seemed to evaporate as I spoke.

As I finished my little introduction and the room settled, the group leader explained what was going to happen. What followed was more like an audition, except in this case without spotlights or stage props. I was asked to give a short demonstration so the rest of the group could evaluate my skill level. This was to be followed by my linking with Spirit and passing messages to everyone in the circle. It felt like my first day at school, with the weight of expectation on my young shoulders. *Wow, I didn't think I was going to be thrown in the deep end this quickly.*

I should point out here for any of you thinking of joining a circle, that in the UK, they take this very seriously, and the format is different in every country. However, before I started, I was told that they were all going to send me energy to elevate my senses.

We started off by reciting the Lord's Prayer in unison, and then they gave me the nod to begin. It was strange for me to be on display in this way, and I felt stripped to my barest essentials as all their eyes watched me intently. I fought to control my nerves and tried to concentrate. I took a deep breath and closed my eyes.

At first, I felt nothing. Total silence. It was as though the outside world ceased to exist for that split second, and I was just in that room. Time seemed to stand still. Nothing else seemed important. Initially, I didn't hear the spirits — I just heard my own breathing, which sounded as if it was being played through an amplifier. Of course, my immediate reaction was one of feeling crushed by failure. One of the sitters (a sitter is the person who is being read), a man called Peter, helped me relax. He began to guide me, telling me to raise my consciousness higher. For a minute, I jokingly thought that "raising my consciousness" meant lifting my butt off the chair. Fortunately, no one at the time saw me inwardly giggle. In reality, what he really meant was for me to expand my consciousness to a higher realm while continuing to expand my energy field. This was all so new to me, yet it started to make sense. I felt my body tingle with energy, which I now know is more about vibrations rather than actual skin tingling!

I took another deep breath, and as I did so, the room began to blur. I felt as though someone had stepped in close and was standing behind me, just as you know when someone comes up behind you when you're standing in line at the bank. I didn't dare turn around to look. Before I could even utter a word, the whole group spoke in unison, saying, "Hello, friend."

At first, I hadn't a clue who they were actually greeting. *Did someone walk into the room? Should I open one eye?* Peter immediately interjected, "John, take your time and just give us what you're receiving."

I relaxed and opened my mouth, and to my absolute astonishment, these amazing words of inspiration just flowed from me. I had no idea who was talking or where the words were coming from. This is what I meant earlier about inspirational speaking. Slowly, I began to recite what was being given to me, and to this day, I can recite the words as though it were yesterday. Here they are:

> *"Many people think strength is a rock or a tall tree,*
> *but the strength of the human heart is immeasurable.*
> *The sun bears down on you, with the light in which all things grow.*
> *Fear not when the cloud passes the sun, for you will know*
> *that the cloud will pass.*

*We are coming through to you with a fluidity of a strong essence.
Come forth and begin."*

No one in the room had any idea that as this Divine inspiration
was given to me, I was being plagued by my own doubts and fears
as to whether I had the ability to work as a medium. The frequent
thoughts of *Am I good enough? What will people say?* and *Am I ready?*
constantly played over and over in my mind, and these fears held
me prisoner in my own self-created insecurity. This is why this
specific message meant so much to me. It was a cathartic experience, and one that enabled me to take the next step in making
the commitment to stay in England and continue on a path that I
knew then and there I had to follow. The words that came through
were not those that I would normally use. I grew up in a very poor
section of Boston, gained a good deal of my "education" off the
streets, and although I regret it now, I never attended a university
or college.

During those two special years that I sat in this circle, I gained
a whole new appreciation about the meaning of wisdom and
inspiration. I was constantly amazed and astonished by what was
delicately placed into my conscious mind from Spirit, which I then
delivered to the group, word for word. I was privileged and honored
to sit with such a diverse and experienced group and to be part of
some truly fascinating inspirational lectures. Words of wisdom,
comfort, and encouragement, and glimpses of the Other-Side were
often the norm; and over the weeks, as I developed, I found myself
in complete unison with the circle members. To this day, the one
thing I'll never forget was the feeling of complete love that perme-
ated the circle and would often remain with me for many days
afterward. Sometimes I'd be sitting in a coffee shop, smiling to
myself, and I'm sure people would wonder why I was so amused or
what had caught my eye. Little did they know!

Sitting in the circle definitely helped me increase my psychic
strength and the length of time I could maintain the link with
Spirit. More important, I now know that this circle was preparing
me for even bigger challenges ahead. During those early months

in the UK, I'd heard about the Arthur Findlay College, which was devoted to Spiritualism and the development of psychic sciences and mediumship. Those lucky enough to attend this unique school would be taught by experienced mediums who traveled there from all corners of the world. I affectionately referred to this school as "Spirit Boot Camp," and of course, once I found out more about it, I couldn't wait to enroll in one of the courses. It was literally a handful of weeks later that I arrived at the college for the first of many classes.

One afternoon we were informed that it was time to give an inspired speech on an unrehearsed subject. We were all going to be "put on the spot" in this way so that we could connect with Spirit and be inspired by our guides. To practice this technique, we were each asked to choose a card with a single word printed on it. Then we'd talk about the subject to the group for several minutes.

When it was my turn to reach in and pull my card, I chose the one that said "Gift." I was blown away by the significance of this card and treasure that moment to this day. I looked at the word again, closed my eyes, and felt Spirit draw close. I tried to put my own thoughts aside as I created space in my mind. I relaxed, and didn't analyze the words that came out of my mouth.

*"Your gifts are like a rose unfolding.*
*You cannot force the bloom.*
*When the rose is opened,*
*then and only then,*
*will you feel it, smell it,*
*and finally, touch it."*

My tutors and fellow students knew that I'd succeeded, because they hadn't heard me talk like that since I'd arrived. Again, the words weren't those I normally used, yet they felt so right at the same time.

This exercise is a great way to start practicing at home. You can try this on your own or with friends by putting several words into a hat and then giving an unrehearsed speech on the one you pick. The first few times you try it, you might draw a blank — or you might find yourself waxing poetic on a subject that's foreign to you. Just speak from your heart, let your guides assist you, and tap into the inspiration you feel at the exact moment you draw the card. More often than not, wonderful things will happen.

Even though it has been years since I lived in the UK and sat in a circle, inspiration still flows through me when I'm lecturing, no matter which country I'm visiting. It's often strange how inspiration comes. When I was giving my first lecture to a packed audience in Sydney, Australia, within minutes of walking onto the huge stage, I was somehow able to connect with that audience in a way that made them feel comfortable with me, and me with them.

Even at night, while I'm watching television, words often start downloading into my mind out of the blue. It's like a computer on some kind of auto setting. It's not as though I'm thinking about a certain subject or even focusing on anything in particular; I'm simply zoning out and watching TV. Words just form and quickly turn into sentences. I notice that this often happens when I'm working on a new book. It's almost as if my guides are still working when I'm not. My friends often laugh at me when they come to my home, as I have pens and scraps of paper or my little voice recorder scattered all over the house. I never know when the words are likely to appear, but I just wish that my guides would choose the earlier part of the day to do this, instead of late at night when the last thing on my mind is recording information that's being given to me. I feel they do this when my mind is tired and I can get out of my own way and give them easy access. I can't complain — after all, they are my guides, my teachers, my friends, and I know they just want to help me. Obviously they keep different hours than I do!

### Viva Las Vegas

Socrates once said: "I decided that it was not wisdom that enabled poets to write their poetry, but a kind of instinct or inspiration, such as you find in seers and prophets who deliver all their sublime messages without knowing what they truly mean."

Inspiration played a big part for me in the spring of 2003. One warm evening I was surprised to receive a phone call from the well-known psychic medium John Edward. I'd met him once before at one of his events in Boston. He'd heard that I was attending, and he'd called me up onto the stage and introduced me to the audience. Of course, I was a bag of nerves walking onto that stage, waving my arms up and down and bowing to him jokingly.

So that night when he called, he said that he was thinking about putting together an event: *John Edward & Friends in Las Vegas,* and asked if I was interested in taking part. He then asked me what the largest audience I'd demonstrated in front of was. I told him it had been about 800. He was quick to respond, "Well, John, how do you feel about 2,000?!"

I mumbled back, "Um, yes . . . that should be okay."

He filled me in a bit more about the event, we said our good-byes, and he was gone.

I was excited, nervous, and anxious all at the same time, as it was the next big leap of faith in myself. By agreeing to do an event with John Edward and two other mediums in front of 2,000 people, I knew this was a test to see if I could take my mediumship to the next level. The weeks flew by, and before I knew it, I found myself touching down over the bright lights of the Las Vegas strip.

I got to the convention center and was informed that I'd be going on second. I was relieved that I was not going to be the first one onstage the next morning. I sat in my hotel room for a while, thinking how much I wanted to be the very best I could, and I hoped that my guides would be there to assist me. I knew they would be, but I also knew that if I allowed my nerves and fear to take control, they could potentially paralyze spirit communication.

The next morning I was searching for something to inspire me and to lift my soul as well as those of the 2,000-member audience. It's always the medium's job to maintain the energy in a demonstration. If you can get the energy and inspiration up, then the messages from the Other-Side flow with clarity and precision.

On the other hand, if the energy is low, then it's even harder for a medium to receive the messages. Most people don't realize that spirit communication is a group effort. One of my popular trademarks is when I call what happens a "three-way conversation." It's a bit like a conference call between Spirit, the medium, and the members of the audience. Each part has to be in sync to make a good connection to help the information flow. Just think how hard it is to get three people in one room to agree on what to have for dinner!

I was called to the greenroom an hour before I was to go onstage. As I walked in the room, not only was John Edward there, but also Reid Tracy, the president of Hay House. I was surprised to see him since I didn't know he would be there. I was one of the new authors with Hay House, my first book *Born Knowing* having just come out, and Reid had never seen me demonstrate before, so he'd flown in to see how his "new guy" was able to hold his own on the big stage. I felt that old pressure of wanting to please everyone and not letting anyone down. It felt like a lot to handle at that precise moment, as I could sense the muscles in my stomach tighten. I knew that I had to go find my inspiration to help me link with the Other-Side.

I'm sure that a lot of people think that before I walk onto that stage, I'm backstage chanting while lighting incense, or even putting myself into some sort of trance. That's not really my style, as I prefer to use music to uplift my energy and my soul. A student named Dee, whom I'd met in the UK, used to listen to the inspirational gospel tunes from the soundtrack of *Sister Act* with Whoopi Goldberg. I remember her telling me once, "If that doesn't lift your spirit — nothing will!" Of course, I always try to clear my head of all the mind chatter as I meditate for just a few moments to make room for the spirit people. I just have to get out of their way, so it becomes less of me, and more of Spirit.

I grabbed my disc player and opted for the upbeat song "Lose Yourself" by rap singer Eminem. The lyrics are all about getting lost in the moment, taking a chance, and going for it because an opportunity may never come again. I knew this was *my* opportunity, and with more than 2,000 pairs of eyes, not to mention John himself;

Reid Tracy; medium Suzane Northrop; and the other participating medium, Robert Brown, all watching me closely, I needed this particular melody to inspire me.

Suzane went on first and wowed the audience with her fast and furious delivery. The audience loved her. As I peeked from behind the curtain, I could see that she was touching people's hearts and lives, as they were wiping their eyes with tissues. I got the five-minute nod. I went back to the greenroom, sat quietly to calm myself, and began to do a short meditation, saying a prayer to God and reaching out to my guides.

Before a demonstration, I often make an initial connection, which seems to be the starting point for the evening. Often before I even arrive at a lecture, I'm aware of some spirit wanting to connect with a loved one. There has been many a time when I've been in the car and looked back to a crowded backseat, filled with those from the Other-Side. You can imagine that this freaks out the driver, wondering who I'm looking at. For someone to grab my attention way before the actual demonstration usually means that the spirit has a really strong personality, in order to get my attention so far in advance. Then again, there are times when I don't have any sort of link until the start of my mediumship demonstration. It's different every time, and that's what makes it so special, yet so unpredictable.

As I sat there in the greenroom, I started to receive information in a series of images. In my mind's eye, I saw what seemed to be a piece of paper being furiously folded. Were they trying to show me a paper plane, a paper toy, or was it just a cutout doll? I was just about to walk onstage, so I tried to interpret what I was receiving as quickly as I could. It finally turned into a beautiful origami swan. (Origami is the Japanese art of folding paper into shapes.) I knew immediately that this was the link. When I receive an image (rather than just words or feelings), I know it's true when they say, "A picture is worth a thousand words." I had no idea who was going to get the message, but I trusted that it would find the right recipient.

I put my music back on for a few seconds to raise my energy to match the level that Suzane had created onstage. I paced back and forth backstage, sweat beginning to form on my brow as my spirit quickened. I often educate my audience about how I raise my energy in an attempt to blend with Spirit, as they lower theirs. It's what I call "the quickening," which I mentioned earlier. This is when the link is strongest.

Every time I walk out onto a stage, I'm aware of the hundreds of faces in the audience, each one looking to me for hope and reassurance. I know that only a few will be chosen, but not directly by me. Some people sit there with their arms folded, jaws clamped shut, and a look on their faces that says, "Prove it to me." Believe me, I can *never* prove it to them. All I can do is give the best evidence I can. Of course, there are those anxiously sitting on the edges of their seats, ready to grab on to anything I say in the hope that it's for them. My advice for these folks is: Don't *reach* for the evidence. Let the medium do his or her job.

Suddenly I heard John Edward announcing me, and I was on. Putting any fears behind me, I strode confidently onstage and gazed out at the audience. The atmosphere was electric as I gave a short talk about myself, how I work, and what people could expect, as well as what *not* to expect. I could feel my energy rising, and conscious that I had less than an hour left, I couldn't wait any longer. The image of the origami swan jumped back into my mind, and at that very moment, I felt a young boy draw close. I knew immediately that this swan was the link to his family. I could feel myself being pulled to the top balcony, so I raised my hand and said, "I have a boy here calling out to his family. He's so excited to be here and wants to talk to his mom! Would someone in that area understand an origami swan?"

Almost before I'd finished speaking, a woman stood up, frantically waving her hands back and forth and yelling, "Up here, John, I think it's for me!"

I always make sure people are not reaching for the message, so I asked her, "So you lost a son?"

"Yes!" she cried out.

"Then you understand the origami swan?" I asked her.

To an almost silent audience, she told how her son had suddenly died a few years earlier, and how a friend had given her an origami swan in remembrance of him. She'd even brought the little folded swan to the event and had it in her wallet. All eyes were focused on her as she reached in and revealed the beautiful paper swan. You could feel the love that was being sent to her at that moment from each and every person in that audience.

Later, I found out that in the Celtic tradition, a swan symbolizes the soul — the aspect of all beings that is eternal. I've since heard that the woman now receives these precious paper swans from people all the time, and every time she receives one, it's like a hello from her son.

My soul was filled with energy that special day because I'd sought inspiration to help me raise my energy to meet those on the Other-Side. Spirit had infused me with its own love, enabling me to pass on hope to those people in Las Vegas. I wonder if John will ever know the kindness he showed by asking me to be part of that event, joining him and the other mediums. This event boosted my confidence to continue my work as a spirit whisperer. Thank you, John Edward.

### Finding Your Inspiration

I firmly believe there are two things that motivate people, one being *inspiration* and the other being *desperation*. Sometimes people are in pain or they're hurting so much that they're forced to do something out of desperation. By the same token, there are people who realize that change is often instigated by inspiration. Let me tell you a beautiful true story.

There's a young couple living in my neighborhood who are the very model of health and wellness. To me, they're an inspiration to so many young couples starting out in their married life, so I asked them if I could use their story to inspire others. Elizabeth is a high school teacher and a freelance personal trainer. On top of this, she also teaches classes at the local gym, and she's a keen jogger. She's super fit. It seems that every time I look outside, she's speeding past my front door riding her bike. Her husband, Allen, is a highly competitive cyclist, and he's constantly entering marathons. His basement is full of impressive-looking bikes, neatly hung on supports. He's up at the crack of dawn almost every morning to squeeze in some jogging, come rain or shine. He's totally committed to his fitness regimen, and just like his wife, is super fit. As I've grown to know them better, I've been so impressed by their ability to balance work, rest, and play.

My life by comparison is more complicated due to my speaking schedule and the constant traveling. I have to carve out time for the essentials of life, for my family and friends, as well as the mundane day-to-day chores. Add to that the ongoing writing, lecturing, and meeting private clients, so it's not surprising that I forget about *me* in the process. I use this only as a comparison to Allen and Elizabeth. The point here is simple: Remember that you have the choice to *live* your life, or *life* will live you! It's always *your* choice.

Watching Elizabeth and Allen live their lives to the fullest, making time for themselves, keeping their bodies strong and healthy, eating well, and getting to travel to remote locations on their quest to experience the wonders of the world has given me renewed inspiration. It's been a timely reminder to start taking care of myself more. Elizabeth encouraged me to get back to a regular exercise regimen, to watch what I eat, to relax, and take breaks when I need them. Hearing her voice in the back of my mind made me commit even more, and it's strange how we respond when we know someone is watching over us. Trust me, I know it's not easy when we're living busy lives! So many of us seem to be on autopilot and push ourselves far more than we should.

If you need inspiration in your life, then don't give up. Go out and find it. I seem to discover inspiration in so many things, just as I have done with my neighbors. I even find that the smallest thing can motivate me. For example, I might see a child playing or overhear a conversation at the supermarket, or it can be as simple as a line from a movie or TV show that just resonates and acts as a catalyst to inspire me to take action. Often, this happens when I am just daydreaming, without really paying attention to anything in particular. You never know when inspiration is going to come knocking at your door.

My colleague and fellow Hay House author Sonia Choquette is one of the most inspiring and motivational speakers I have ever witnessed. We're often on the same circuit, and I've seen her lecture to packed audiences all over the world. Her principle is based on: *Move your body — to move your soul!* She frequently brings her musician friend Mark Stanton Welch to accompany her, with his upbeat music to motivate her audience. Even the most inhibited people who would never dare to stand up with everyone else and dance are encouraged to get to their feet, move their hips, and shake every inch of their bodies. It's amazing to watch her call upon a sad soul who has low self-esteem, someone who's riddled by the fear of being noticed, and see how she intuitively tunes in to their positive traits. She exudes such positive energy and manages to bring these people to the front of the stage, where she gets them to sing, dance, or even yell at the top of their lungs. Audience members walk away with their souls vibrating. If we could all just feel that way, I believe we could change the world.

Try to surround yourself with those who inspire you, challenge you, and encourage you to step out of your comfort zone. After all, these people are likely to give you the strength and courage to reach further than you've attempted to reach before. You really notice this when you work with like-minded individuals, as it's so much easier to blend and resonate with each other, not just mentally or intellectually, but with your heart and soul. When you're inspired, it fills you with a sense of power and purpose. Inspiration is a powerful force, and it provides the energy that will motivate you to push yourself further. These are the times when a goal or a desire is actually within your reach!

If you've been suffering from boredom, feeling listless and tired, or just not caring about anything or anyone, then most likely you're feeling a sense of *desperation* to change something, and *inspiration* can be that catalyst for change. First and foremost, try to find something that inspires you. I've listed a few things in the following paragraphs that may inspire you. Be daring and challenge yourself; you may want to even try something new, something scary that pushes you outside your comfort zone. It could even be something you always wanted to try but never had the nerve or the time to do.

Inspiration is not solely linked to success. Last year I took motorcycle lessons, and although I didn't pass, it gave me a feeling of accomplishment to be able to say, "I did that." I'd always wanted to drive a motorbike and had visions of racing around country lanes, and even though I failed the test, at least I tried.

By comparison, years earlier I took scuba-diving lessons, something I'd always wanted to do. Yes, that time I did pass the test, and that day will remain in my heart and soul for the rest of my life. I remember the invigorating feeling as I nervously strapped on my air tanks and took my first plunge into the ocean, looking at the spectacular underwater world that God created. I often draw on this memory as inspiration, and it's helped me through some tough times when I feel I need that boost, but most of all . . . hope.

Find what motivates you, whether it's music, dancing, singing, drawing, or even getting back to nature. No matter what it is, you'll know it when you find it! Give yourself the opportunity to change, to make your life better, to make even *more* of who you really are. When you feel inspiration filling you with positive energy, you'll realize that you can in fact change. When I'm nervous about doing something, I just tell myself, *I can do this!* Everyone's different. Focus on what *you* love doing, and before long, your soul will start to sing and help you reach your full potential.

Let inspiration fill your soul and allow it to motivate you — it's a lot more satisfying than desperation.

# CHAPTER 4

# TRANSFIGURATION — THE FACE OF SPIRIT

"Am I really seeing what I think I'm seeing?" I turned and whispered to one of my fellow students and teachers in the packed lecture hall. It was eerily quiet, and I could feel the intensity of the atmosphere as everyone sat on the edge of their seats staring at the medium. I was lucky enough to be part of a private gathering where a Transfiguration Medium would demonstrate his extraordinary ability. What with all the reading I'd done on psychic phenomena and mediumship, I couldn't wait to see this specialized type of mediumship for real.

During my intensive two-year stay in England, where I studied every aspect of mediumship, I was privileged to witness many strange yet wondrous demonstrations of the extraordinary power of Spirit. Of course, I'd heard about this type of mediumship, but never thought I would get to attend an actual demonstration, since this form of mediumship is actually very rare and takes years of dedication and patience to develop on the part of the medium.

A gasp rippled through the audience as the faces of the dead started to overlay the face of the medium onstage. If I hadn't witnessed this with my own eyes, I might not have believed it! It was an extraordinary experience.

## *What Is Transfiguration?*

Before I finish this story, let me explain a bit more what this is all about. Transfiguration is a rare form of mediumship that allows those in spirit to materialize, and communicate through the medium. To put it in the simplest way, it's when the face of the person who has passed on appears over the face of the medium. I know you're most likely saying to yourself right now, *What?!* So let me explain further.

A Transfiguration Medium has the ability to communicate (like other mediums) with those in the Spirit World, but something different also happens. Anyone who has seen me work knows that I talk about raising my energy (which, as I mentioned, I often refer to as "the quickening"), which is all part of blending my vibrations with those of Spirit to forge the connection.

Transfiguration Mediums start out in the same way. First, they enter a trancelike state or an altered state of consciousness. Then, when the time is right, a veil of ectoplasm slowly appears in front of their faces, and it's this veil that gets molded into the exact features of the spirit who's trying to communicate. When I witnessed this for the first time, I must admit that I did say to myself, *John, keep an open mind here, and experience the whole thing before you react, or decide on what you feel you've seen.*

Ectoplasm is a translucent substance that oozes from the medium's body during the trance state. Spirits are able to manipulate and use the substance to push their own faces through the veil just like a mask. It's not remotely gory or anything like that; and once spirits have communicated, the ectoplasm returns back into the medium's body. The substance is very light-sensitive, and that's why many Transfiguration Mediums will often hold séances in darkened rooms.

In the UK, transfiguration was very popular during the late 19th century and the early part of the 20th century, when interest in Spiritualism was at an all-time high as a result of the horrific human loss resulting from World War I. Thousands of people became interested in the whole concept and the reality of the afterlife.

Grieving families tried to come to terms with the loss, often spanning generations, as fathers, husbands, and sons were lost during the war. So many people with broken hearts wanted to know if there really was an afterlife and if their loved ones were safe.

I found it immensely poignant when I read how people who'd lost loved ones in the First World War would attend transfiguration séances, in the hopes that they would get the opportunity to see their loved ones' faces just one more time. I know from doing this work that all too often when someone dies tragically, such as in the case of war, the family members who are left to grieve have a harder time coming to terms with their loss, as they rarely get the opportunity to say good-bye.

Nevertheless, I do want to reiterate that this form of mediumship is quite rare. It takes absolute dedication and desire as well as patience to sit in a development circle for years to aquire this special ability. Therefore, you can imagine that when I was offered the opportunity to witness this myself, I jumped at the opportunity.

### February 1997

My friends in the UK used to laugh at the way I often described British winters. Being from New England, where we could often get many feet of snow in any one winter, you'd think I'd be used to the cold. British winters are so different, as I could see on that late afternoon when I looked out the cold frosted window from my upstairs bedroom. The heavy gray clouds seemed to be especially low, and I shivered as I pulled on my coat in anticipation of going outside. I'd been waiting (with a sense of excitement about what was to happen later that day) for my fellow student Bruce to pull up outside. He'd offered to drive some friends and me to the much-anticipated event to watch our very first transfiguration demonstration. I was the first one to be picked up. Little did I know that I would be personally touched by that special evening so long ago.

We collected everyone along the way, and after driving for what seemed like forever, we pulled up outside the hall. As we walked in, I immediately noticed the hundred or so chairs that were lined up row after row in perfect order. Of course we were early, because I'd been insistent that we get there in plenty of time, as I wanted to sit as close as possible to the stage. The hall was like an old school building, with high ceilings and draped windows. Nobody spoke very much, and when they did, it was in hushed whispers. It was eerily quiet, which added to the sense of anticipation.

We managed to get a full row of seats on the left-hand side about seven rows back from the small stage. The stage was stark, with nothing apart from one single chair positioned in the middle of it. A red spotlight cast a pool of soft, warm light over the chair. That was it! I looked at Bruce and asked him, "Why is there a red light shining on the stage?" I was told that once the medium took the stage, the normal hall lights would be dimmed to near dark-ness, and the only light that could be used for the transfiguration had to be in red, so as not to interrupt ectoplasm from forming.

I was taking everything in, looking around me, but from where I sat it was clear that there were no contraptions, curtains, trapdoors, or mirrors anywhere in the area — just this simple stage and a chair! Even though I was a student of mediumship and psychic sciences, I always made sure that I came with an open mind, but at the same time, I'd keep my logical, rational mind in the forefront.

The hall slowly filled until almost every seat was taken. I was acutely aware of the muted whispers and murmurs around me. There was clearly some trepidation in the room, as everyone was twitching in their seats and anxiously waiting for the medium to walk onto the stage. The organizer finally stepped onstage and told us what we were about to witness, and asked us to be as quiet as possible so the medium would not be disturbed as he went into trance to begin his demonstration.

The medium stepped onto the stage to be introduced. I had no idea what to expect, but he appeared to be an average man, maybe a little short, but big in girth. He was completely bald and had a kind smile as he said hello to the audience. He gave a little introduction, telling us that it would take a few minutes for the trance to take over, and he thanked us for our patience. The lights were dimmed, and he sat almost motionless in a pool of red light that illuminated his upper torso and face.

As my eyes grew accustomed to the lower light level, it was possible to see the outline of his body and the edges of the stage through the dimness of the red light. You could have heard a pin drop. It was as though everyone had left their coughs and colds outside. At that moment, he closed his eyes and the whole audience seemed to hold its collective breath. Within minutes, the medium seemed to slip away from us; even the very air seemed to change, as if a spiritual force was now coming forward. I was mesmerized.

It was one of those experiences when you know there are other people in the audience, yet you feel as though it's just you. Everyone in the hall had surely noticed a change. The ectoplasm from the medium's body created a mistlike veil over his face. The only way I can describe it here is that it was as if I were looking through dirty glasses. I'd hardly noticed it appear, it was so subtle.

As I stared ever intently, his own face seemed to disappear as though it were fading away as he looked out at the audience. I know we were told to remain absolutely quiet, but I couldn't hold back as I turned to one of my friends. "Am I really seeing what I think I'm seeing?" I whispered. It reminded me of driving in thick fog, where you find yourself staring harder and harder in an attempt to find some recognizable shape. As I stared more intently, I noticed that through the veil a face was slowly forming with what looked like a long thin beard and a long mustache. As the eyes started to develop, the first thing I noticed was that they were slanted. It was clear that I was now seeing what looked like an elderly Chinese man. His features became increasingly prominent. As a reality check here, it's important to remember that the medium was white, bald, and had a heavyset body. What was in front of us now was an Asian man, and the normal contours of the medium's face had all but disappeared.

As I stole a quick glance around the audience, I saw that most of the people were wide-eyed themselves — jaws dropped and heads tilted — probably wondering if they too were really seeing what their eyes were being shown. Did I need to pinch myself? I shook my head several times to make sure my eyes weren't playing tricks on me. I looked to my left and right, and in a whisper asked my friends what they were seeing. I wanted to make sure we were *all* seeing the same thing.

"What are *you* seeing?"

They both mouthed back at me, "A Chinese man!"

This man actually turned out to be the medium's guide, who spoke to us for some time, giving the most wonderful inspirational speech on spirituality.

It was as though time stood still for me that night, yet I was aware of the evening progressing as more and more faces came through one by one, each time calling out with specific names to people in the audience. For many of the audience members, their loved ones' faces were coming through and speaking to them with messages of love and support and the validation that they still lived on. When I've delivered a special message, it usually confirms that I'm following the right path, and I'm sure this medium felt the same, as mothers and fathers were being reunited with their children, husbands or wives were once again seeing their sweethearts, and old friends were getting a unique chance to say hello to each other.

I was transfixed and amazed by what I was witnessing. The emotions of the people who were receiving messages were overwhelming as everyone opened their hearts and souls to the spirits coming through, and you could feel the years of pain and bereavement somehow slip away. I know that many people were blessed with healed hearts as well as the closure they so much needed on that particular night.

For me, I was just happy to be there and to take part in this extraordinary evening. I'd pretty much gone in with an open mind and wasn't expecting what happened next. As the previous face disappeared, a young man's face started to materialize, the hairstyle changing from a long, straight, full head of hair to short, spiky hair that stood upright like the way kids wear their hair today. The eyes became wider, and the face had prominent cheeks. I continued staring, because somehow this face looked vaguely familiar to me. At first I didn't connect. The medium appeared to roll his head ever so slowly from the left to right and seemed to stare in my area as if he were looking for someone specific in my section.

He called out ever so quietly at first, "John? . . . John, are you there?"

Even his voice seemed to take on a younger tone. Could this be a message for *me?* I looked at my friends, who nudged me to speak up. I looked around to make sure nobody else was about to respond, then called out in an uncharacteristically shaky voice, "Is it me you want? I'm John!" I was actually excited, thrilled, and nervous all at the same time. The face of the young man had completely formed, and he slowly started to speak.

"Hello, John. It's me, Michael. Please tell them that it was an accident and I didn't mean to do it."

I could actually see one single tear roll down his face as he said, "Thank you, and please tell them I love them so very much."

I was unable to hold back the emotion as tears trickled down my cheeks, too. One of my friends reached over and held my hand, not really understanding the nature of the connection.

I looked back with wet eyes, my voice now even shakier.

"Yes, Michael, I will tell them everything I've seen and heard this evening, and God bless you," I said, trying to hold back the greater flow of tears I knew was trying to make its way out. Michael's face began to fade as another one was coming through for someone else in the audience. That's all he really wanted to say. It was short and to the point.

The experience that night is one that will remain with me for the rest of my life. Little did anyone know that I'd received a call less than two weeks before this event, telling me that one of my dear friends back home in Massachusetts had lost her only brother, Michael, who was younger than she was. He was a good kid who had lived life to the fullest, was never short of friends, and was a much-loved son and brother. He was also a good friend of my youngest sister, as they had gone to school together. He lived just across the street from my family. Sadly, in his teenage years he got involved with drugs, and from that moment on could never seem to get his life back on track. Michael was found dead from a heroin overdose. When a friend of his called me, he said that Michael's family hadn't been informed about the true cause of death, so they never actually knew if it was a heroin overdose or a suicide attempt.

That night, even though I was more than 3,000 miles away in a different country, Michael came through to bring whatever comfort he could to his family by telling them that his passing was indeed an accident, and he'd never intended to end his life. I think he knew he could use me as a conduit to get the message back to his loved ones, and most important, to deliver it in a sensitive and compassionate way.

Even as I write this, the emotion of that night and the message imparted is surging through my body again. Being a few years older, I'd watched Michael grow up from a young boy playing in my backyard with my sister; enter high school; and eventually become a good-looking, kind young man. He was always there with a big smile and piercing blue eyes whenever he greeted anyone. When I moved to California, I lost touch with him and his family, except for the occasional phone call from his sister.

After the event, I had to think long and hard about how I was going to pass on this information. I thought that I should probably call Michael's sister and let her pass it on to the rest of her family. We knew each other pretty well from having been to the same school and often found ourselves at various social gatherings together throughout the years. She was pretty relaxed about my psychic sensitivity and accepted it as part of who I was without any judgment. I decided to wait one more month, since her brother had just passed. I knew that the family would be in shock and pain due to his unexpected passing.

I remember the day I called his sister. She just listened intently to what I told her and was touched by the message that came from her brother. She thanked me profusely and said she would pass on the message to the rest of her family. I whispered softly on the phone to her, "Don't thank me — thank your brother."

I just recently spoke to Michael's sister again, and she told me that her brother has visited her in her dreams. I also know that he has appeared in the dreams of other people he knew who had their own issues with drugs. I feel that Michael is somehow reaching out lovingly, trying to help and warn people here about the dangers of drugs.

I truly believe that no matter how someone passes or how long ago it happened, we're never separated from our loved ones. Neither distance, time, nor death can ever separate us — we are and always will be connected to each other. Love is truly everlasting.

# CHAPTER 5

# LIVING IMAGES —
# PSYCHIC ART

I passionately believe that art is a true expression of the soul. The world of art in all its forms, particularly in the use of color, has always held a fascination for me. Often as a child, I would retreat into my own private world, and curl up by the window with a box of crayons and anything else I could find that would help me express what I was feeling or seeing. My hands seemed to take on a life of their own as they sketched images, symbols, people, and places I realized I'd never known. Sometimes, it was as if time would just stand still, and I'd find myself drawing into the wee hours of the morning. My mom would find me hiding under the bedcovers, sketching by the light of a small bedside lamp. When I began to draw, it was as though the outside world somehow faded away, and in its place another magical world opened up to me. This was a place I could escape to, one where I felt safe, and most important, a place that didn't care if I was "different." Yet in all this, somehow it was always welcoming.

Of course, I took art classes in elementary school, where I was taught how to use different colors, learned how to finger-paint, and how to stay within the lines! Even at that early age, my artistic ability went far beyond what other children were doing. Looking back, I often wonder if I was born with an overly developed artistic gene. Did I inherit it from one of my ancestors? Perhaps I'd been an artist in some past life? Or maybe those in the Spirit World were inspiring me, even though as a child, I had no perception of such things?

When something needed to be drawn, it always seemed that my teachers or fellow students would come to me! "John, can you draw this for us!" or "John, I need a horse drawn." I was the one who won all the college-sponsored competitions, and my wall was adorned with ribbons and certificates. I remember when I was disqualified from an art contest sponsored by the Boston Museum of Science because I was accused of having my mom or dad do the drawing. In reality, I don't think I'd ever seen either of them put pen to paper apart from paying bills!

Even today, when I get a few minutes to myself in my busy schedule, I love to while away a few hours in museums or stroll around art galleries. It's sort of my time to inspire my soul with my "creative fix." I take in all the colors and brushstrokes; and absorb the feelings and emotions that the sculptures, pictures, and paintings evoke in me. Art has been and always will be a feature of my life and a big part of who I am. My only regret nowadays is that I don't have enough time to do my own artwork, whether it's pastels, charcoals, sculpting, or even photography. I know . . . I guess it's more about choosing to simply make the time. It's so important to find time, as you can't get it back once it's past.

A friend of mine who lives an equally busy life is passionate about playing the piano. He has so little time that the only way for him to enjoy his music is to schedule it as though it's a business meeting. He literally blocks out time in his calendar so that he can play. I guess that works for him! So, if you're passionate about art, photography, or anything creative, and you find you just don't have the time, why don't you try his approach and make a date with yourself to feed your soul? Aren't you worth it?

### *Watching the Masters at Work*

Living in England for those two magical years in the late 1990s while I was studying and developing my mediumship, I was able to witness the many different ways in which mediums work. Being in a country where there seemed to be an art gallery or museum on almost every corner, and with stone buildings that were hundreds of years old, it seemed that each stone could tell its own story. It was a dream come true and a feast for my creative soul, apart from just my eyes. Having thrown myself into researching everything and everyone, I'd heard about one woman who was renowned for her work in "psychic art." Since I love anything to do with creativity, I made it my business to find out about this talented artist and medium. Who was she, how she did work in unison with Spirit, and most important, where did she work?

There are many different ways in which Spirit works through those who have the ability. Some psychic artists let Spirit control their hands as they begin to draw, while others go into a deep trance and let Spirit completely take over, more often with their eyes completely closed! Others see images in their mind's eye, which are probably given to them. In such cases, they simply draw what they're seeing. Over the years, I've discovered that many psychic artists have little or no formal training; or in some cases, they have no actual artistic ability at all. Yet once the link is established, their guides step in to assist them in drawing works of art they'd never be able to do on their own. To this day, I still find this process absolutely fascinating.

I was sitting at the kitchen table one evening after dinner and started scanning the local newspaper. I saw an advertisement for a demonstration with two world-renowned mediums, one whom I'd grown to respect for his books and the integrity of his demonstrations. His books had played a part in my own learning as I was developing my mediumship. His name is Stephen O'Brien, and a psychic artist named Coral Polge — whom I'd heard so much about — was going to be joining him. Coral was an established and talented artist; and in the beginning of her career, she said she didn't believe in mediums. The irony was that she'd been told by more than one medium that someday she would be serving the Spirit World as a psychic artist and would be world famous. As a result, she'd begun to experiment in the privacy of her own home in a psychic circle, where she'd started developing her ability. Nothing daunted her, from the simplicity of drawing just a few lines to completing complex portraits.

It wasn't long before she was able to draw one of her Spirit Guides, Maurice de Latour, who was believed to be an 18th-century portrait painter. Sadly, Coral passed away in 2001, but I was privileged to see her work in person that night. Being an artist myself, I knew that I had to try to book a private session with her and get my own spirit drawings. I remember thinking to myself that since she was so popular, she'd be completely booked up, and getting an appointment was pretty unlikely.

Coral would sit with clients, tune in with those on the Other-Side, and draw their loved ones who had passed on. She would actually just draw what she was seeing. Spirits would show themselves to her either as they were when they passed, or come through showing themselves at whatever age they chose. Her drawings were amazingly accurate, as they resembled loved ones so clearly that many clients would gasp due to the uncanny likeness of the spirit person.

People would excitedly run home to find pictures of the deceased and compare the drawing that Coral had just done with the old photograph. It was almost unsettling, as though she'd been looking at the very same photo! She also developed a reputation for being able to draw people's guides, letting each stroke of her pencil or pastels create the images she was inspired to draw. She could not only draw deceased loved ones and guides, but at times she would comment as she drew, giving accurate information about the person she was drawing.

During her lectures and demonstrations, Coral would say that drawing people who'd passed on wasn't that easy. I know all too well that it can get a little confusing, especially when the information is garbled or when there are too many voices vying for your attention at the same time. I've been known on many an occasion to tell an audience, "It's getting a bit crowded up here!"

For Coral, the spirits would often come through younger, which meant that the recipient would have to validate the portrait by finding a long-lost photograph. On those occasions when several spirits were trying to communicate simultaneously, she'd find herself drawing the top part of the face of a grandmother, and the bottom part of a grandfather, as the two faces fused together. I once read a lovely story she told about a time when she'd drawn a picture of a certain man. The woman she was linking with wasn't able to recognize the drawing at the time, but Coral's work is so beautiful, and the woman loved the drawing so much, that she decided to frame it and hang it in her hallway. One day a new neighbor was visiting, and as the woman walked into the hall, she glanced at the new picture on the wall. "Where on earth did you get a picture of my father?" she asked in utter disbelief. When Spirit wants to get something to someone — they know how to do it!

In the end, Coral gave more than 50 years of dedicated service to the Spirit World and to those here who were fortunate enough to receive one of her drawings, which helped thousands truly understand that their loved ones survived death and still live on.

+·❉·+

Going back to that special evening, which had been billed as "An Evening of Mediumship & Psychic Art," Stephen and Coral had worked together many times; and I was thrilled to see how the two would work in tandem delivering messages as well as the drawings. I went with my usual group of friends; and arriving at the venue, we found people descending from everywhere, scrambling to get inside to grab a good seat. When I walked in, hundreds of chairs in the auditorium were already filled. The stage was already set with a single microphone, an overhead projector, and one of the largest projection screens I'd ever seen. The place was abuzz with voices chattering and people twitching in their chairs in anticipation of the evening. The atmosphere was already fully charged. We found some empty seats in the center of the auditorium, not too far from the stage. It was strange, as it was as if these seats were waiting just for us! The following account is taken from my memory of that wonderful evening more than 13 years ago, and it's just a part of the many extraordinary readings that happened that night.

We'd barely sat down before the announcement began: "Ladies and gentlemen, welcome to an evening of mediumship and psychic art. Please put your hands together for two of Britain's most hailed mediums: Stephen O'Brien and Coral Polge!" The place roared with applause, and the two were given a standing ovation. The night hadn't even begun!

Coral came out, bowed graciously, and walked over to the stool beside the overhead projector. She would draw on transparent sheets of plastic that would be projected on the giant screen for all to see. As she composed herself, Stephen took center stage and began to explain how the two would work: "Ladies and gentlemen, thank you so much for being here, and welcome. Coral and I hope that we can assist you today and be of service to the Spirit World, as well as to all of you here this evening. I'll be linking with those in the Spirit World, and Coral will pick up on the same link. I'll give the messages and describe whom I'm receiving information from, and Coral will draw the spirit that we're both connected with. So that's how it should work."

The audience was spellbound, and everyone sat in silence, listening as Stephen gave his speech. I've seen two mediums pick up on the same link of a person who has passed many times since that event. It's a bit like when you have more than one phone in the house, and someone picks up the other handset so that they can chat at the same time. It's really awesome to witness when it does happen, not just for the recipient of the message — but also for me! With Stephen giving the message and Coral drawing the spirit, it certainly made it much easier for the spirit to reach out to the person he or she was trying to contact. For those in the audience that night, they not only got to take home a message, but had the bonus of a drawing as well. What a great gift, and one that I'm sure they treasured.

Stephen paced back and forth, and I knew he was beginning to connect with a spirit on the Other-Side. At the same time, Coral began to draw as though someone had turned on some hidden switch. They were clearly in sync! On the projection screen, a face was already appearing, and gradually as she added detail, it took shape. The atmosphere was electric, and Stephen wasted no time before he pointed to the back of the audience and said, "I'm coming to the back section. I have someone's mom here, and she's telling me she's been gone for quite some time. She's giving me the name Anne, and she's telling me that she passed from cancer that went to the brain." He barely stopped to take a breath before carrying on. "She's saying her daughters are in the audience. As a matter of fact, two are here, but one couldn't come, so you had to give the ticket to someone else." The audience was totally enthralled by this time, and I was fascinated to see someone else work like this. He clearly had a strong link. Brilliant!

Coral had already drawn the face of a woman before Stephen had even gotten as far as saying it was a mom. He really never stopped for a second to glance behind him to see what Coral was drawing, but standing at the very front of the stage, he continued delivering the message, talking faster and faster. The soft lines Coral was adding were detailing the woman's face, the thick hair being drawn in bold strokes. She stopped for a minute and chuckled to herself, looked up, and joined in, "Stephen, this woman's telling me that I've drawn her hairline too high and to lower it." The audience murmured with amusement at the details coming from these two mediums. "She's quite particular about how her hair was, and it has to be just right!" Coral went on and began to add more hair as the hairline dropped, under strict instructions from the woman. She looked up again, and this time raising her voice for everyone to hear, said, "This woman has the most beautiful blue eyes and was well known for them."

All eyes were on Stephen and the big screen, as the woman's face became almost lifelike. While it felt as if many minutes had passed, it had only been one or two in reality. I was aware that two women in the back were waving their hands wildly in the air, trying to get Stephen's attention. Runners scampered up the stairs to hand microphones to the women. They both grabbed ahold of them, standing up with excitement, eyes full of tears. They desperately tried to suppress their sobs as they explained, "That's our mother, Anne! It's her. She passed more than 15 years ago. Our other sister couldn't come tonight, so we invited a friend instead."

The second sister, who seemed desperate to speak, picked up the story, "Our mom had really beautiful blue eyes, but none of us were lucky enough to inherit them." She took a deep breath as she said, "Yes, she did pass from cancer; and yes, it did go to her brain. Coral's drawing is exactly how she looked before she started to get ill. It's quite uncanny. She was so particular about her hair right up to the time she passed. I guess she still is!"

The audience all laughed, and so did the mom's two daughters. It seemed to ease the tension. They were laughing and crying at the same time as they realized that their mother really was there and was still part of their lives. Coral was still drawing furiously as she continued to add earrings, clothes, and buttons; and she fixed the hair yet again so it looked perfect. She would erase a bit, then go back to the face to raise an eyebrow or fix the lips before she finally added the design to the woman's silk blouse. I knew at that moment that I was watching two masters at work.

Stephen continued, as more information came through, with exact names, professions, dates of birthdays and anniversaries, and even nicknames. He confirmed (which was validation of the message) what the family was doing at the time, and some of the events that had happened since their mom passed, with both women screaming in unison, "Yes! Yes! Yes! Oh my goodness!"

The audience was clearly loving what we were all witnessing, and you would have had to have been a hard-nosed skeptic to not believe what you were watching that night. Watching the two of them work together was not just an education and an honor, but helped me to strive to set the bar even higher for the work I knew lay ahead of me.

The atmosphere in the auditorium was filled with excitement and love as Coral continued to draw psychic portraits. Stephen forged more links with Spirit, giving accurate validations for each message he delivered. People were crying, laughing, even screaming as the messages and drawings were paired with someone in the audience. It's strange as I write about this event that took place so long ago, since the memory is as fresh as though it happened yesterday.

The evening finally started to wind down, even though I was wishing that it would go on forever. Seeing the smiles and tears of joy as we filed out — and not just on the faces of lucky recipients of the messages — was a treat for me. I think that everyone benefited from that evening, and I'm sure it gave them hope that their loved ones were still alive and well on the Other-Side. I'll always remember the mediumship, the detailed validations by Stephen, and the beautiful drawings by Coral. That one special night left an indelible imprint on my soul forever.

Walking home that evening, I could never have suspected that I'd have an opportunity to sit with Coral myself. How wrong I was!

### The Sitting

I truly believe that synchronicities and so-called coincidences are clear signs that Spirit is knocking on your door. Sometimes it can be a soft tap, or for those times when you're not paying attention, it can be a loud bang! Spirit working through synchronicity can manifest itself in some unique ways. I refer to them as my *Divine nudges*. I'm sure that synchronicity played a big part in getting me a personal reading from Coral Polge.

What's really strange is that I'd been in the UK for some time, but I hadn't really stopped since the day I'd arrived, throwing myself into my work, networking, going to circle-development groups, and watching mediums working in the churches — not to mention my study trips to the Arthur Findlay College. Months had quickly slipped by, but I wasn't complaining, so I thought it was about time I became a tourist. As much as I was enjoying living in Bristol, this industrial city steeped in Victorian architecture in the southwest of England, I wanted to see more. After all, it was only two hours by train to London. I needed a break from it all, just to put a bit of perspective back into my life. One of my favorite sayings is: "We're spiritual beings, but we're also physical beings, and we should honor both."

Too much psychic work would often leave me feeling ungrounded, as I constantly used my upper energy centers, better known as *chakras*. I wouldn't pay enough attention to the lower energy centers of my body to keep me balanced and grounded, as I knew this helped me remain connected to the physical world. I needed to do something physical and colorful, so I researched the many buses and trains that would get me to London. I know it sounds a bit clichéd, but I had always wanted to see Buckingham Palace, where the guards stand like mannequins without a movement or letting anything break their cold stare. I'd also heard about Trafalgar Square and so many other sites!

I was going to get an artistic overload by exploring some of the museums and art galleries. I'd heard so much about these amazing buildings and their treasures! I had to admit that I was excited, knowing that I was going to get up close to original pieces of art by masters such as van Gogh, Monet, Picasso, Gauguin, and so many others. The richness of the architecture was an art form in itself, what with the Houses of Parliament with their gray stone, and the imposing tower of Big Ben that set off the London skyline.

It was hard to believe that I'd been in England for more than four months and hadn't ventured outside Bristol. I'd justified it to myself, saying, "John, you're here to study, not play!" I didn't know how long I was going to be able to stay in England, so I wanted to use every chance I could to develop my abilities.

Again, synchronicity had its hand in helping to further my plans. Out of the blue, a friend of mine said he had some business in London, and asked if I would like to come along and have two days to explore and do a bit of sightseeing while he was in meetings. As if I needed the invitation — of course I jumped at that chance! Although I'd promised myself some downtime, I also wanted to visit the Spiritualist Association of Great Britain (SAGB), which had been set up in 1872. The association moved to Belgrave Square in London in the 1940s, where it still thrives, serving the principles of the Spiritualist movement. It's a fascinating place to visit, and seems to be forever holding classes and lectures. I'd read about all the paintings of mediums from bygone days and the historical building itself, so I knew I couldn't pass up the chance to pop in. I didn't plan to take a class, but just to visit this place while I was touring the other sites in London.

We got to London, and I was duly dropped off. The first thing that hit me was the sheer volume of people of almost every nationality. Now I really felt like a true tourist, with my backpack and tourist map, which I clung to as I headed off toward Belgrave Square. I thought that I'd do that first, and spend the rest of the time enjoying myself. I think the smile on my face was more about me, feeling rather proud of myself that I was navigating my way through London — all alone! Anybody that knows me well will tell you that I'm totally useless with directions and jokingly classify myself as "directionally dysfunctional."

As I entered the white pristine building of the SAGB, people of all ages were milling around, some by themselves, while others were in small groups. I looked at the impressive selection of books, stuck my head into one of the lecture halls, and examined the pictures of some notable mediums who had paved the way for those of us to follow. While I was looking around, checking out every corner of the place, I noticed a woman come up to the front desk and say to the clerk that she was ready for the next reading. I looked again, and to my disbelief, it was Coral Polge! She was there just for the day doing spirit drawings. I couldn't believe that she was there at the same time as I was. I wished I'd known in advance, so I could have tried to get an appointment. I knew they were booked well ahead of time, as she was so popular. Of course, I'd had no idea that I was going be there, since the whole trip was unplanned.

I was about to walk out when synchronicity took me by the hand one more time. I guess by that point I should have been getting used to this! As I stood there, in a slight daze, I noticed a nice-looking woman enter the lobby, holding a few of the portraits that Coral had just drawn for her. A group of friends was waiting for her, and the woman excitedly showed off her artwork. I could overhear them speaking of the exact likeness of the woman's relatives.

Oh, I could feel the tug. Part of me really wished I were holding those portraits. I watched in awe as Coral took her next client to the little back room. That was it. I couldn't resist and turned around and walked back in. I inquired at the front desk how long she would be there. "Well, young man, she's only here for the day," I was told. The clerk noticed my disappointment, looked at her schedule, and said, "But you know, here's a strange thing. I've just taken a cancellation!" Coral had one opening left in two hours.

My excitement must have lit up the whole reception area. I couldn't believe I was about to sit with the most famous psychic artist in the world. I hardly knew what to think, so I took myself out for lunch with the idea of seeing another tourist spot, but I only had one thing on my mind. I sat down to eat a sandwich and thought about how everything had miraculously come together — starting with my friend suddenly asking me to go to London at the spur of the moment. What were the chances of someone canceling like that? Somehow, I believed this was meant to be and that Divine timing was playing its hand in getting me that appointment. I was totally psyched.

Two hours slipped by in a heartbeat, and before I knew it, I was back in the lobby for my appointment. After reading about Coral and seeing her work onstage some months earlier with Stephen, I could barely contain my excitement and enthusiasm. *Okay, calm down, boy!* I said to myself, as Coral greeted me at the front desk and escorted me to a small, comfortable room, where there were two seats and a small table with her drawing pad and the many different multicolored pastels that looked like one big beautiful rainbow of colors.

We exchanged greetings, and she immediately noticed my American accent. I told her I was from New England. Coral radiated the kindest energy, which seemed to spread throughout the room. It left me feeling wonderfully calm and relaxed. We both sat down; and she took a moment or two to gather her thoughts, took in a deep breath, and began, launching straight in. "You know, dear, that you're psychically gifted, yes?"

"Yes, thank you, Coral," I replied. I didn't want to give her any leading information. I knew as a student medium that we prefer not to be given any information from the person we're sitting with, or information about those on the Other-Side, unless it's to validate a piece of information given by the medium. I was trying to practice what I preach.

Without any fuss or hesitation, Coral picked up her pastels and started to sketch. *How exciting is this!* I thought. My mind went into silent overdrive, wondering who she was linking with and what face I was going to see staring back at me. She must have read my mind, as she spoke and drew at the same time. "John, you know that I'll draw more than one!"

A few minutes later, I saw that her first drawing was an elderly Italian woman. She said that she felt it was probably a great-grandmother and that she'd lived in Italy. My mom's dad, my grandfather John (whom I'm named after), did in fact emigrate from Italy to America. I never met him, though, as he died suddenly when my mom was a young woman. I was sure that this had to be his mother.

Coral had carried on drawing while she was talking about my family, where we'd lived, and the different names in the family. She occasionally looked up at me, and then beyond me, as if the person was posing for her in person. I had to struggle not to turn around myself and take a peek. Pastels were being chosen, erasing done here and there, shading in of one area, then darkening of another. As an aspiring artist myself, I was fascinated to watch her work, and realized that she was getting her inspiration from somewhere, too. She simply just drew and talked as if we were old friends. I couldn't see the portrait from the angle in which she held her drawing pad. Eventually, she said she was finished, and when she turned the drawing pad around, before me was the face of my great-grandmother.

The drawing was beautiful, and although I'd never met her, she looked like a simple Italian woman from a small village. She was elderly-looking, with small, dark, purposeful eyes; wrinkles in all the right places; and a handkerchief that covered her hair and was tied in a small knot under her chin. Her spirit had chosen to come through as she was in her older years, rather than as a younger woman. The validations Coral gave me were all correct, but I would have to check with my family the next time I spoke to them to validate the portrait, since I didn't have any knowledge of my grandfather's family, or even if there were photographs of this woman back home.

Coral then adjusted her seat, and once again put pastel to paper. "John, I'm picking up one of your guides," she said. "Did you know that you have a Tibetan monk as one of your guides?"

All I could do was nod my head as I uttered a rather feeble, "Yes."

It dawned on me that a few months earlier I'd been at a mediumship demonstration when a medium singled me out and said, "You, young man in the back, you a have a lovely man standing behind you, and he's one of your main guides." I heard his voice in my head. "Your guide is a Tibetan monk," he'd continued. "He's working with you and says that you are exactly where you should be at this point in your development. His message is quite simple, it's this: 'All you need to do is let go and trust.'" It all came flooding back in an instant. Once again, the Tibetan monk makes an appearance!

I remember sitting there in that small room at the SAGB in London, thinking, *What better place to be introduced to one of my guides and having Coral draw him, too!* Of course I'd read a lot about spirit guides, but this was just the evidence I'd hoped to receive. As I mentioned earlier, I remembered that as a child, I'd often dream of praying men with shaved heads and colorful robes. Now, I realize that they were Tibetan monks . . . and one of them was actually *my* guide.

As he linked with Coral, the Tibetan monk was about to have his face captured on paper. I was suddenly acutely aware that the atmosphere seemed to change in the room. A sense of total peace washed over my entire body, and I could feel the emotion of pure love wrap its arms around me. I could tell that my guide was sending his thoughts to Coral as well as to me. She continued to draw and talk to me at the same time.

"John, you know he's been with you throughout your life, and he's been assisting you with your mediumship and acting as a teacher for you in this lifetime," she said.

As she was drawing, all I could think about was how I've always been drawn to Tibet, the beautiful Himalayas, and had vowed someday to visit this extraordinary country — which is called "the roof of the world." It's not just a mere statement. The valley bottoms of Tibet are higher than the highest mountains elsewhere. I don't know why, but even today, I really feel as though I lived there at one time, and most likely that I might have been a Tibetan monk myself. It's all too familiar to me not to believe that, as I seem to resonate with the country as well as its people.

Coral was almost finished. She gave me more information about where Spirit and my mediumship would take me and the work that I still had ahead of me. The image of my Tibetan guide touched me as she handed me his portrait. I was almost moved to tears. His eyes are what I noticed the most. They were the gentlest eyes I'd ever seen. They seemed to reach out and touch my very soul. His face seemed so familiar. At that, I felt a single tear trickle down my face. My emotions were flooding to the surface as I realized that this beautiful man had been with me my entire life. Somehow, he'd always been there, never intruding or demanding, but gently guiding me. Coral asked if I was okay.

"Yes, Coral, I'm just filled with so many emotions right now — first just having the honor of sitting with you, and now seeing the face of my guide for the first time," I told her.

"I know we all have guides, but somehow having this experience was what I needed at this very time in my life." I went on to tell her how I was living in the UK, far away from friends and family. I even told her how I'd spent some time recently wondering whether I was doing the right thing. Part of me questioned where this work was taking me. Seeing my guide's face for the first time put it into perspective and somehow made it all the more real. I felt a sense of ease as all my fears melted away. Once again, here was the lesson I had to learn — namely: let go and trust.

I was about to get up, but she said she had one more drawing of another guide who really wanted to introduce himself. I didn't need any persuasion. She went straight to it, pastel to paper, telling me that this time he was an African shaman and that he'd also been with me for a long time.

"He's telling me, John, that it's his job to protect you and to give you the strength to get through difficult times in your life." Twenty minutes later, she showed me how he'd chosen to come through, with the face markings being that of how an African shaman would typically paint his face. He was a big man, but like my Tibetan monk, he had an amazingly friendly face that just stared back at me. Now I know why I have so many African masks and art pieces hanging on my walls back home. I gain an inner strength when I look at them.

Many times we find ourselves drawn to pieces of art, particular foods, or the architecture of a specific country. We don't know why we like these things, just that we do. Maybe a past-life memory is surfacing or it's just that our guides are influencing us. As I stared at the portrait of my African guide, I realized that he'd been influencing me for some time. It was just that I hadn't stopped to listen and acknowledge where the influence was coming from.

My time with Coral was just about to end. I got up to say good-bye with portraits in hand. I thanked her profusely and began to walk toward the door, knowing that another person was waiting for a sitting. She looked at me and said very sweetly, "Keep up the good work, young man."

I turned back and said, "I will now . . . knowing that I have plenty of help. Good-bye and God bless you."

The drawings that Coral did of my guides are prominently displayed in my meditation room, which also doubles as my studio for my weekly radio show. I think she'd be happy to know that I'm being watched over when I'm on air! They add to the atmosphere and instill a sense of calmness within me every time I glance at them.

Coral will surely be missed by the thousands here who have witnessed her demonstrations of psychic art, and by those like me whom she has touched personally. I hope that right now Coral is working with someone here, inspiring him, and assisting and guiding him on a path that lets him know that we're all eternal, that we existed before we were born, and will go on long after we leave this physical body. Just as we have special friends here, so do we in the Spirit World.

# CHAPTER 6

## THE CHILDREN

"Will you help us?" The voice was clear and strong, and then I heard it again.

"Will you help us?"

Where was this voice coming from? I could hear it so clearly, yet it didn't sound like an adult voice, more like that of a child. Then it dawned on me: it *was* children, lots of them, all talking in unison. I could see dozens of children's faces appearing before me, ranging from toddlers to young adults. They were of different nationalities, and of course all shapes and sizes. Yet it was so strange. It was as though they spoke as a collective, speaking with one voice — one thought.

They'd all come to me in a dream many years ago. The only words I'd heard telepathically were those asking for help. I knew this was a visitation from some of the many children in the Spirit World. They were clearly reaching beyond the veil and into my dreams. I stood there in my dream, looking at their faces asking me for help, and all I could offer was a single-word answer: "Yes."

As I was getting dressed the following morning, the impact of the dream was strong, and as I was processing it, I realized that these children were asking me to represent them. They knew I could help! They would use me to speak to their parents, friends, and families. I had one burning desire for them — to make their wishes come true! After all, that was my job now, and in the years that followed I was able to help many.

Some dreams come and go, while some make no sense at all, as if your brain is simply clearing away issues — or is it more about creating space for the important ones? It's these dreams that are often the most profound and can be an After Death Communication (ADC). These are the dreams that seem to stay with you forever. That morning, I knew from this dream (which happened when I was first developing as a medium) that it was very real.

In those early development days, while still living in Los Angeles, I worked a full-time job and did my psychic work whenever I had the chance, usually in the evenings and on Saturdays. Word of mouth seemed to be spreading fast, and I was quickly building a waiting list of people eager to have a private reading. The inquiries kept flooding in. I had an ongoing inner battle, concerned that I would not be able to support myself financially if I devoted my whole life to service, yet the calling was so strong.

It was a constant conversation over supper with my usual group of friends. "I'm just one man," I would say. I repeatedly questioned whether I wanted to live the life of a medium. Did I have what it took to help so many people, and would it drain me physically and emotionally? The questions played over and over. I knew that when the time was right, the decision would probably be made *for* me, as opposed to *by* me. I had no idea that the sign would come so soon, and so clear, but it did! It all changed when one little spirit girl tapped her way into my heart.

### Jennifer

Those who have seen me speak or have read my books will know this story, but it's so touching that it's always worth reading again. It all happened shortly after I got back to Los Angeles after those two magical years in England. I'd taken a full-time job working for a temp agency in the city. It was strange going back to a nine-to-five routine, but I needed the money, and in my spare time I would see people for private sittings.

A young woman named Melinda had left several messages asking to see me while she was visiting Los Angeles, and of course I'd agreed to see her. As busy as I was, I could psychically feel her pain. I just knew I had to make the time.

She sat quietly across the room from me, and a full lineup appeared, with numerous relatives stepping forward one by one. In the background, I was acutely aware of a faint tapping that I was psychically hearing. It was just there. I know this might sound stupid, but it sounded as if someone was lightly running and gliding across a polished tiled floor. It was confusing. It wasn't the familiar rhythm of a waltz or even a song that I could recognize, yet there it was again — a definite rhythm. It sounded more like *clackity-clack, clackity-clack, clackity-clack.*

*Oh my God, heaven is actually tap dancing,* I said to myself.

At that moment, a little girl stepped forward and gave me her name. She was so excited. *Go, go, go . . .*

I didn't hesitate a moment longer. "Melinda, I have a little girl here, and she is giving me the name of Jen or Jennifer. Do you understand that?"

"Yes, John, that's my daughter!" she exclaimed, with her hand quickly going to her chest.

Melinda's eyes instantly filled with tears. I could tell that once again I'd succeeded in becoming a spirit whisperer for someone from the Other-Side. For a split second, I wondered whether this little girl had been one of the children asking for my help in that dream. I really hoped so.

Jennifer was Melinda's five-year-old daughter. She'd tragically died after a kidney operation on Father's Day. Melinda was able to tell me through her tears that the hospital staff had begged her and the rest of the family to "go home, relax, and get something to eat" — just for an hour — because nothing would happen. Yet something awful *did* happen.

Lisa, Jennifer's seven-year-old sister, was running through the overgrown grass in the front yard at the exact moment that Jennifer passed. Her parents found Lisa pointing upward, crying, "See! My sister! My sister!" to a small white butterfly that swooped down and slowly circled over Lisa's head.

As Melinda and I sat there, I felt her pain and the depth of her sadness. Three years had passed since Jennifer's death, and Melinda had come to see me with one burning question. She needed to know if her baby was safe in heaven. I wanted so terribly to give her some answers, but at first I felt frustrated, as I couldn't *see* or *feel* Jennifer. Instead, I just kept hearing the same noise, over and over . . . *clackity-clack, clackity-clack, clackity-clack.*

I realized that I couldn't ignore the sound any longer, so I asked her, "Melinda, did Jennifer take tap-dancing lessons?"

Melinda started weeping again. "No, but I understand the sound," she whispered. "The Christmas before Jennifer died, she received a pair of clogs that had metal heels on them, which tapped when she walked.

"The shoes were really too big for Jennifer's little feet," she went on, "but she insisted on wearing them anyway, even though they almost fell off with a clacking thud every time she walked. In fact, Jennifer loved those shoes so much that she'd often beg me to visit her aunt who worked in a hospital with endless hallways of highly polished tiled floors, so she could skip down the long corridors for maximum effect. John, she adored the *clackity-clack* noise, which echoed down the hallways." Melinda looked at me, and I could see the love in her eyes.

"You know, John, she would often ask me, 'Do you hear me making the noise, Mommy?'"

This was one of those readings where I struggled to hold back my own tears. Melinda told me that Jennifer loved those shoes so much, she decided to bury her in those shoes.

"You know, Melinda, I hear her dancing in heaven," I said, and as I did so, I could feel the link fading away, but Jennifer had one further message for her mother: "Please tell Mommy that it doesn't hurt anymore, and I love the balloons."

Melinda was speechless. She took a few long breaths and composed herself.

"On the anniversary of Jennifer's death, and on her birthday each year, we stuff balloons with a message for her and release them into the sky. We put her name and her photo on each and every balloon!"

I had this wonderful image in my mind of masses of balloons going up to heaven. What an amazing reading. I was drained. So was Melinda, but in a good way.

I had to go to the beach to clear my head and recharge my soul. It was quite late, and I was the only one out there. I sat down in the sand to watch a brilliant sunset. As I stared off into the horizon, I couldn't help but notice something bobbing just off the shoreline. I kicked off my sneakers and walked down to the water. I couldn't believe my eyes. There was a single red balloon. It was as though a personal thank-you had been sent via special delivery . . . compliments of Jennifer. I sat on the beach for a while longer, holding the red balloon.

Readings like this make the work I do all the more worthwhile and constantly give me validation, confirming that I'm in the right profession. I didn't realize at the time how many people use balloons in memory of their children. Nowadays, every time someone sends up balloons to honor a child, I receive the words: *balloons to heaven.* This was the title of Jennifer's story in the opening of my first book.

I really feel that Jennifer continues to help me when I work with parents who have lost children. As a result of that reading with Melinda, and the way that Jennifer touched my heart, I knew right at that moment that I *had* to continue with my spirit-whisperer work, and probably devote 100 percent of my time to it, rather than splitting it between two jobs. In a way, the decision *had* been made for me! Those cases where someone loses a child are the ones that touch my soul and pull on my heartstrings the most.

+ ⁑ +

The love between a parent and child is one of the deepest and most precious connections we make during our time on Earth. Children start out as part of us, and upon uttering their very first words, they establish themselves as the biggest parts of our hearts. We dream of watching our children grow up, be able to stand on their own two feet, and become independent, because it's the natural order of things. Of course, parents want to leave the planet before their son or daughter makes that final journey, so it's hard to understand why life doesn't always cooperate and a child is taken prematurely to the Other-Side.

When this happens, a parent is often left with more questions than answers, such as: "Why did this happen?" "Is the universe a fair place?" "Are they alone?" "Who's taking care of my children now?" "Were they in pain when it happened?" "Do they know how much we love them and miss them?"

Sadly, no one seems to want to talk about the death of a child because they fear it will make the grieving parent feel even more uncomfortable. My work brings me into contact with many desolate parents who've told me when they've lost their child how other family members and friends are nervous about mentioning the boy or girl's name because they think it may cause further pain and distress. Yet many parents tell me that they'd be happier to be able to talk about their son or daughter, to revisit happy memories, and to hear their child's name once again.

As we grow up, we learn the basic rules of life: how to live, how to love, and how to acquire things. However, we don't really learn what to do when we lose children. That's why many who've suffered a loss decide to seek out a bereavement counselor, which I highly recommend; and under the right circumstances, a medium can also assist in this process. I would not recommend going to a medium immediately after a child passes, as the process of bereavement has to be honored, and the parents need time. I also believe that those who have passed need to get used to being back in the Spirit World. It works both ways.

I couldn't write this book without touching on just a few of the standout readings that I've given to some wonderful parents. I know that I can't bring their children back physically, but with their help, I try to show them that their children are still alive and well in the Spirit World, and that they're never alone. It doesn't matter if a child was a toddler or an adult; he or she is and always will be the little girl or boy a parent loves and remembers.

### Nick's Gift

I've been going to the Omega Institute in Rhinebeck, New York, for many years to lecture, teach, and demonstrate my mediumship. It's a holistic center offering innovative educational experiences to awaken the best in the human spirit. Their mission is to provide hope and healing. Every year I take part with other facilitators in a weekend entitled "Soul Survival." There are four of us who lecture about near-death experiences, reincarnation, and bereavement, as well as the continuity of life. It's truly a spectacular weekend; and people come from all over the world to receive knowledge, wisdom, and hopefully a connection with their loved ones. It was here that I met Janet, who was attending the event.

She'd sent me a beautiful letter after that weekend, and something must have touched my heart, as I agreed to speak to her. We had a good talk on the phone about her son Nick and how he'd unexpectedly passed at the all-too-young age of 25. She'd told me that he was too young, vibrant, and strong to have left them so suddenly. He was a boy with a smile that could light up a room, had no problem meeting girls, and had many friends who adored and looked up to him.

The doctors ruled Nick's death as heart failure due to natural causes. Janet's family was in total shock when it happened. Even though he'd died three years earlier, she still needed healing, longed for some type of closure, and very much wanted to contact him. Again, it was one of those situations where I just I knew I had to see her family, and so I invited them to New Hampshire to see me personally.

I remember the day very well. It was one of those typical humid August days in New England, where the whirring air conditioner was doing all it could to keep out the hot, sticky weather we'd been having all week. Janet was a lovely, kind woman, yet the look on her face as she walked in was one of relief that she was finally there. She'd driven nonstop for more than five hours from New York. Following right behind her was Nick Sr., a large Italian man who looked like he'd stepped right off the television show *The Sopranos;* along with Nick's younger brother, Mike, a quite good-looking young man. However, he was very quiet as he followed his parents into the room.

I left the room for a few moments so they could get settled and knew it wouldn't be long, as their son Nick was waiting. I'd felt him for some time. His love for his family was strong, and he was anxious to reconnect with them. I walked back into the room and gave my usual little speech about how I work, but it wasn't long before Nick spoke up.

"Nick's quite excited, and he couldn't wait till you got here," I said, feeling his energy swirl around my whole body. "You know, as I was driving here from my home, he told me to take his name and somehow put it with some type of stuffed bear. Do you understand that?"

The whole family sighed with relief. The tension eased a bit and everyone relaxed, knowing that Nick was there.

Nick Sr. laughed as he said, "Yes, my son was such a big kid. I used to joke with him all the time by calling him a Berenstain Bear, the bears from the famous children's books."

"He loved that!" I continued as Nick chattered away fast and furiously.

"I'm supposed to acknowledge a female here, probably a girlfriend, and somehow it's tied to this month of August. It's her birthday month, and oh yes . . . he's telling me it's very close to his birthday, too!"

It was wonderful to watch the family bask in all the happy memories as Nick talked about sailing on the water, as he knew how much his family still enjoyed boating.

"Nick says he saw you on the boat. Do you understand?"

"Yes!" they all said together.

"Well, guys, he still enjoys being with you on the boat, and you should know that he's right there with you all."

As I was linking with Nick, I could so feel his personality and mannerisms, and I noticed that I was running my fingers through my hair just like he did. I could feel his sense of humor and his self-assuredness. At 25, and being so popular and good-looking, who wouldn't be confident?

Janet noticed me pushing my hair back. "That's our Nick!" she said as she wiped the tear from her eye.

"I'm supposed to tell you that his temper has calmed down. I'm assuming that you understand, yes."

Nick's dad simply said, "Oh yeah. He did have quite the temper, John."

I felt a slight shift in energy. Nick became a little more serious, and I felt he wanted to talk to his family about his actual passing. "He's telling me how sudden it all was. He had no time to say good-bye to anyone. I feel this is his time to do that now — not that he's gone forever, but he really wants you all to know he's fine and still watching over you."

I told the family that many people wonder what their loved ones are doing on the Other-Side. "Nick wants me to tell you he's working with children here as well as over there."

Janet and Nick Sr. took comfort in knowing that in life their son loved children, and it was amazing how they gravitated to him. They were obviously delighted that he was continuing to work with them, albeit in spirit.

At this point in the reading, nobody seemed to care how hot it was in the room. We were all glowing nicely. Yet Nick hadn't finished, and prodded me to look over at his brother, Mike.

"Mike, I met your girlfriend downstairs, and she's in the waiting room," I said, and immediately went on to tell him how Nick keeps that fantastic smile. "You know, Mike, he's telling me to say to you, 'I'll be at the wedding.' Does he mean *your* wedding, Mike?" I grinned at him.

"Well, my girlfriend's sister is getting married. Maybe he means that?" Mike tried to sidestep the question, shifting attention away from himself. Nevertheless, his dad would have none of that.

"Or . . . it could be *your* wedding," Nick Sr. said proudly, as if he knew more than his son was letting on.

I was still blending with their son's energy. Nick wasn't letting up. He kept mentioning a name that sounded like Daniel, Dane, or Daniela.

"Who has a name like Daniel or Daniela?" I asked.

Janet spoke right up and told us that their friend Daniela made a special memorial for Nick. The family was really touched by it.

"Nick wants you all to know that he still sees what's going on with his friends and family. He's still very much a part of everything! He's calling out to someone named Bobby."

Nick Sr., who was hanging on my every word, said that Bobby was one of his best friends. I reminded him that even though these individuals are not here in the physical world, they still hold all their memories and friendships very close to them in the Spirit World. After all, it's the people in our lives, and the memories that we share together, that helps make us who we are.

It had already been well over an hour, and Nick's link was still loud and clear, so as it was the last appointment of the day, I continued with the reading. I told the family that I felt sure Nick must have been strong when he was here, as he was so strong in spirit.

"Dad, he's telling me that he saw you fix the chandelier last week," I told Nick Sr.

I had to make sure I stayed strong for them. It would be easy to get emotionally involved. When that happens, I can't be of service as a spirit whisperer.

Nick Sr. said, with a quiver in his voice, "Oh my God, how could you know that I just fixed the chandelier last week?!"

"Well, I didn't know until your son just told me."

I told them that when spirits come through, they talk about how much they loved their family members, but I push the spirit to give me all the little things that happened to them and to the family after they passed. I find that the little things can be far more significant, and are what people appreciate most. It's all part of the validation and goes a long way to allowing some closure to take place, especially in this case, where Nick had died so suddenly.

I had the bizarre sensation of my head tickling, and I could almost feel Nick rummaging around in my mind and my memory bank. I suddenly remembered when I was hit by a car when I was three years old, and I saw myself there with my leg cast. Because of the accident, one of my legs is now a little shorter than the other. I guess it was Nick's way of bringing a similar incident to light.

"Was Nick hit sometime ago by a car?"

His dad was still wiping his tears, "Yes, he was."

His brother, Mike, who had been pretty quiet throughout, chimed in, "John, his foot was hurt so bad that he had to have metal pins put in to support it."

Janet and Nick Sr. held hands as they just kept shaking their head back and forth. The link was so clear, and it was obvious that Nick was still in full swing.

"I know your son's got a sense a humor, because he's showing me . . . what's this? Are there memories of a snake?"

The whole family laughed through their tears.

"He keeps repeating to me, 'The snake escaped! The snake escaped! Say it, John, please!' Why would he say that?"

Nick Sr. spoke up, laughing loudly. "Because it *did* escape! We got a snake from our neighbor. I think it was a water snake. I bought a brand-new car, and we put the snake in a little box in the car. The stupid thing is that he got loose in the car for weeks. We would come out and see it sunning himself in plain sight, but by the time we could get in, he went back under the seat. We finally caught him. We always laughed about that."

"Well, Nick is a wonderful communicator. After all, who else would know that?"

"No one would know that, John, just us. I can't believe he's bringing up the story of the snake!" was all his surprised dad could say.

There were many other validations that day, too many to put in writing. There were also some that were quite personal, just for the family to hear, which I've chosen to omit here out of respect. Finally, before we all collapsed from heat exhaustion, I could feel Nick's energy fading, but true to form, he showed me one more thing that stood out among all the validations.

During my training as a medium, I was taught that you should give what you're receiving. If you don't, then you might misinterpret what those in spirit are trying to really say to you. So I continued, and gave the family what I was being pressed to give. In my mind, I was seeing the exact section of my book I'd written the previous night, which is included in the "Inspirational Mediumship" section of this book.

"You know . . . Nick is showing me the exact story for the new book I'm writing," I went on. "I stopped last night at the part where I gave a message about an origami swan to someone at one of my lectures. I'm going to finish writing the story about this woman who received paper swans from people when her son passed, and how the swan represents the eternal part of the soul."

I went on, as I had to know why Nick was getting me to talk about this. "I really think I'm supposed to ask you if an origami swan means anything to you, also."

At this point, Nick Sr. looked at his wife, she looked at him, and Mike looked at both of them in disbelief.

Janet began weeping and smiling at the same time as she told me about the swans.

"John, a few weeks ago I learned how to make origami swans, and on the anniversary of Nick's passing, I sat by his grave and made many swans for all the people who visit him. I was alone at his grave, and I said to him, 'Nick, if you mention this swan to John . . . I'll know you're still with us and this is for real.'" At that point, Janet reached inside her purse and pulled out one small, beautifully made paper swan she'd created and handed it to me as a gift.

You could have heard a pin drop in that room. We were all overcome with emotion.

"You know, I feel your son actually made me stop writing last night just so he could use that information for today's reading with you all."

The whole family was crying again, because when Janet had pulled the swan out of her purse and given it to me, they'd seen me wiping a single tear running down my cheek.

The love that we felt was all-encompassing, and it ran right through all of us.

The link was now starting to fade away, so I ended with, "Your son and brother still love you; and please remember that neither distance, time, nor even death can separate you all, because love is truly everlasting."

As they all got up to go, I hugged each of them one by one. That special swan now sits proudly on my mantelpiece. Every time I look at it, I think of Nick and his family and how those in Spirit will do everything in their power to prove that their love never ends. That special swan will always remind me of why I am a spirit whisperer, and my special responsibilities, which I will fulfill, until it's my time to go home.

### The Beat Goes On

Suddenly it happens. I'm very used to it and prepared. I know what to expect. I just simply know. Sometimes it's a whisper of words, an abstract image or symbol, or just emotions that flood into my mind. Then there's the overshadowing of those in the Spirit World, when they try to get my attention as I begin to link and blend with their energy. This is the format I use once a month when I do a small group reading for eight people. It's a way in which people can come together and share in their loss. Also, it's a wonderful forum to celebrate the joy as well as the healing that often occurs when people get together who all have the same hope — that their loved ones will come through. It's always a special time for laughter as well as tears. For some it's their last chance to say good-bye; for others it's a time to say hello again.

An extraordinary emotional connection takes place when the readings begin. Everyone listens to each other's messages from loved ones on the Other-Side, and to the responses. I've been involved with these groups for many years now and have seen almost every permutation possible. My approach constantly evolves, and no two groups are ever the same. I never truly know what will happen or who's going to show up. Some people arrive looking nervous or anxious, while others are relaxed and happy. Then there are those who've come alone, feeling isolated from friends and family who don't know how to approach them or simply don't know what to say when they lose someone. One thing has never changed, which is that the support that they get from each other is a beautiful thing to witness.

Guidelines are sent in advance, and I often repeat them as people are getting settled. I tell them what to expect, how I work, and how I need them to focus on not just *who* they want to hear from, but to be open to other people who might show up. When loved ones come through, they're usually never alone. I tell them what I tell everyone, whether it's in this small group of eight or an audience of thousands: I don't choose the spirits — they choose me.

Just a few months ago, before finishing this book, I was preparing for a group. I have a bit of a routine, as I know that these three-hour gatherings are hugely draining for me, so I try to take a short rest in the afternoon to fully charge my batteries. It was early spring, and the air still had the remnants of the winter crispness, yet flowers were beginning to bloom. I had a sense of anticipation that tonight's group was going to be interesting. I lay down, but didn't really rest. Those on the Other-Side wouldn't let me and were beginning to overshadow my own thoughts. They were already starting to make their presence known.

I showered and got ready. The group started off, and everything went as usual until I was reading for an elderly woman who'd lost her husband some years ago. Validations of their life together were being given, but in the background and toward the end of the reading, I kept hearing soft drumbeats. Well, I knew it wasn't coming from the building. It had to be coming from Spirit. It had style and rhythm, starting off quite faintly, but growing louder as time went on. When spirits want to get my attention, they know how to do it. Sometimes they even cut in on other people's readings, and I feel this is exactly what was happening this time. Yet I'm disciplined enough now to have my rules, so I finished the message.

*Bang, bang, bang* . . . the drumming would not stop. To top if off now, I was psychically hearing not just the beat of that drum, but also the clap of cymbals. It was almost as if I were having my own personal concert in my head. With only eight people to choose from, it's a fast track for the link. There was a mother and daughter sitting across from me, and without even realizing what I was doing, I began to mimic playing the drums and cymbals myself! I looked straight at them.

"Who's the drummer, because he's surely making a lot of noise here trying to get my attention?" I asked, hoping that they knew what I was talking about.

Both mom and daughter looked shocked, happy, and surprised all at the same time. I didn't give them a chance to answer.

"Is this your brother?" I said to the younger of the two. The tears immediately trickled down her face, leaving wet streaks as Lauren acknowledged that her brother had indeed passed.

"John, he's using the best way he knows to get your attention," she replied through her sobs.

"Well, he's quite a character, isn't he? He was certainly keen, as he jumped in before I'd barely finished the previous message. He must have been a drummer while he was here, and I can tell you, he's obviously still playing over there."

His sister, Lauren, and his mom, Paula, confirmed that he had been a professional drummer and was a great lover of music and pop culture. They told me that he had an uncanny ability to master any instrument, which made him something of a local legend in his hometown. They looked at each other with excitement and waited for me to continue.

"Now, ladies, you know I don't like to give two names, John and Mary, because they're so very common, and me being half-Italian, half-Irish, and Catholic, these names are not just common to me, but to most people. I'm sorry, but I have to give you what he's telling me. I'm hearing the names John and Mary; do you understand that?"

Paula spoke first: "John is my son who passed, and Mary was his girlfriend."

"Mary is still part of our family and still very involved with us," Lauren said lovingly.

"So much love coming through for you both. Wow! There must be a birthday right now because he's showing me a birthday candle."

"Yes, John's birthday was this week, and he would have been 24," she continued.

I could feel John's sense of urgency, as he wanted to make sure his family knew it was really him! It was funny how he worked, as I could still hear the drums beating softly in the background.

"I'm feeling pain in my head. He's telling me that he was found by water. Is that correct?"

"Yes, he was found with a head wound, on the shore of a beach," they both said in almost perfect unison.

"Ladies, I'm so sorry." I paused to frame the next part of the message delicately. "I have to tell you that I don't feel he passed from a drowning, but rather from the head wound he suffered before he fell into the water. He keeps yelling out, 'I wasn't in pain, Mom; it happened so fast, so unexpectedly but there was no pain!'"

I could see Lauren and Paula breathe a sigh of relief as they wiped away their tears. I'm sure this was one of the main questions they hoped to have answered. Of course, they didn't know that the whole group was sending them their love and strength as the reading continued. They must have felt it, though.

I could tell they desperately wanted to know exactly what happened, but I never did find the underlying cause of what had transpired that tragic evening. It was frustrating for me because he'd given me so much information and specific details on his life, except for the actual cause of his sudden death. No matter how long or how much I do this work, I still don't know why someone filled with so much love, life, music, and creativity is taken from us. Equally, there's no rhyme or reason as to why I don't receive more information on mysterious cases like these. I've learned that I'm just a medium, a man, and that those in the Spirit World have their own agenda, so I have to trust and leave it in their hands.

It's difficult enough when you lose a family member, but it's doubly hard to lose the love of your life. These types of messages are especially emotional for me. John was sending me loving memories of all the good times he'd had with his girlfriend, Mary. He told me about attending concerts at the Hatch Shell in Boston — a stage shaped like a giant shell and famous for hosting concerts by the great conductor Keith Lockhart of the Boston Pops! He talked about a fun trip to Las Vegas that he and Mary had enjoyed, and also passed on additional information to his sister and mom.

"He's telling me, ladies, that he knows how hard this is for you. Also, please tell Mary he knows how much she's still suffering. He wants her to know he's still with her, and he knows she's having trouble moving on. He really wants her to, and he's telling me that she will be able to meet some special people soon, including men, and knows that he will never be replaced. It will just be different. He says that she so deserves to be happy. He's actually saying something to me personally now. Yes, I know."

"Please tell Mary that he just said to me, 'I want that for her.'"

Suddenly, in my mind, I saw a dalmatian dog running free, jumping and happy, and I knew he was with John.

"What's this he's showing me? Wow, who had the dalmatian dog? I've never had a dalmatian come through in all the time I've been doing this work. I've had lots of breeds but never this one! Your dalmatian has met up with John."

All Lauren could do was smile as she said, "Yes, we had a dalmatian when we were kids."

Being a dog lover myself, with my own little Koda, I find it so comforting when people realize that their four-legged friends end up in the Spirit World as well. When it's your time to go home, no matter what, you're never alone.

A few more validations came through before the session came to an end. I repeated to Lauren and her mother how much John loved them, and that he would always be with them. As John stepped back, he gave me one last message.

"Ladies, just one more thing he's saying. He's telling you to expect some special pictures to turn up that you've never seen before." With that, he was gone. Slowly they gathered their things, and everyone in the group shared hugs and dispersed into the night.

It's been many months since I gave this reading, but just the other day John's mom contacted me. She told me that a couple weeks after the reading, one of John's good friends stayed the night with them, and just before he left, he turned to the family, reached inside his bag, and said, "Oh, I almost forgot! The sax player in John's band stopped by and wanted me to give you these pictures."

John's mom said they were the most beautiful candid shots of her son, and some of them you could just kiss. They showed his many wonderful sides — his expressions, mannerisms, and of course, that smile! Her voice trembled over the phone as she said, "I have countless pictures of John, but these were just so special. Now I know why we were told to expect them!"

"Thank you, John," she told me.

"Please don't thank me; thank your drummer boy," I whispered, fighting back my own tears as I hung up.

This story truly resonates with me and speaks to my heart on many levels. It's about a family living through the unbearable sadness of missing a son, a brother, a boyfriend, and a friend. Yet I have to give credit to John's family, for they are the heroes in this story. Through their pain, they've helped many others. After John's death, his family went on to establish the John Ryan Pike Memorial Project, which is an amazing lending library of musical instruments for instructors and high-school students whose music programs have been downsized or completely phased out. It's their goal with this memorial project to eventually create a community of professional and novice musicians alike, interested in learning, sharing, and collaborating with one another. They hope that these people will work together in a creative atmosphere as a sort of

"band." It will not only promote teamwork, but will also be a catalyst for the development of other skills, including but not limited
to mathematics and science.

How proud John must be of his family! Although he may not
be here physically, his spirit will always live on in his creativity, his
music, and the lives he's touched here, as well as on the Other-Side.
He entertained the world with his music, his enthusiasm, and his
love; and somehow I believe he's now playing private concerts for
the angels. With John, the beat truly does go on!

# CHAPTER 7

# UNEXPECTED MESSAGES

One of the constant themes I write about is the hectic pace of life. It's got nothing to do with the commitment to one's work; it's more about how the pace of life overtakes everything else. I notice it wherever I go, whatever I'm doing. Everyone is carrying their mobile phones or some other form of instant-messaging device! Of course, I remember the world pre-e-mail, Twitter, and cell phones. Some of my older friends remember having to use old-fashioned snail mail to correspond, and then there was the novelty of sending a fax before the explosion of instant messaging.

The net effect of all this instant communication is that we're always rushing about, as though there aren't enough hours in the day. We've become more impatient and intolerant, more concerned about results than the journey to get there! These days, we want things done yesterday and expect things to just materialize or happen when *we* want them to. One place where I notice how dependent we've become on our mobile phones is just before a film starts in a movie theater, and you see everyone take one last glance before turning them off. The glow in the cinema says it all.

Over the years since I've been writing, I've had to learn to embrace technology myself, even to the point where I have a blog and a Facebook profile; and yes, I even "Twitter." Yet with a heavy heart, I have to acknowledge that all this technology has had an effect on our well-being. Take a moment to ask yourself, when did checking your e-mail become more important than having a healthy breakfast?

We so rarely take the time to pause long enough to be aware of the beautiful details around us, or take the time to meditate, or even remember that it's okay to simply . . . breathe.

As a medium, I've long realized that Spirit is not bound or constrained by what we know as *physical time,* such as 60 minutes in each hour, 24 hours in each day, and so on. Time, clocks, and calendars are things we've created to keep our lives structured and in some type of working order, but in the Spirit World, the idea of *time* is totally different. It's a popular misconception that the Spirit World is somehow part of our world. In reality, it's the other way around. We are and always will be part of theirs. I may be a spirit whisperer, but when it comes to spirit communication and receiving messages, I know I have to follow their rules. They have their own timing, their own agenda, and their own special way of getting a message to us unexpectedly, just when we need it. Trust me when I say, "When they want to reach out to someone here, they know exactly the time and place, and the perfect conditions for sending the message."

This has happened hundreds of times, but I do remember one instance in particular. It was a day when I wasn't working and just enjoying lunch with my friend Simon and a business associate of his named Carol. Now, she knew all about me and that I was studying mediumship. She'd invited us to lunch, and we were just sitting down to eat when I began to pick up thoughts from her dad who had passed sometime before. Remember, this was back in the days when I was just training, so I hadn't learned to switch it on and off as I can now. I think Carol could see that something was going on and gave me an inquisitive look across the table. I didn't feel embarrassed or awkward telling her what was happening.

In my usual way, I came straight out with it: "Carol, is your mom suffering right now from a throat ailment?"

She looked up and said with surprise, "Yes! She was just diagnosed yesterday with lesions on her thyroid gland! How could you know that?"

"Your dad's telling me that he's aware of what's going on with your mom's throat, and he wants you to know that he's going to be right beside you both through it all." No sooner had Carol's dad linked with me than he was gone. The message was as simple as that. That was it, quicker than an e-mail but so effective, and totally on his terms! Carol just smiled at me, comforted by the information she'd just received, and we carried on with lunch and hardly mentioned it again.

Almost everyone who attends one of my smaller group gatherings or comes to one of the larger demonstrations does so with an expectation of *who* they want to hear from and *what* they even want these people to say. Even in our normal lives, it's rare that we have conversations with such control of the content or outcome. I find it amazing that people believe they can place such expectations on their loved ones. I have little control over who comes through when I do a reading. They choose me — I don't choose them. It isn't a case of 1-800-Dial-the-Dead.

I have many clients who came to see me thinking that those in the Spirit World could solve all their problems. One time I gave two sisters a reading, and their mom came through with plenty of validations of the lives they shared together. She let them know that she was aware of what was going on in their lives since passing. At the end of the reading, one of the sisters let out a heavy sigh. I asked her if there was something wrong, and I remember her replying, "John, I was hoping that my mom was going to tell me whether I should divorce my husband or not!"

Of course, I had to tell her that's *not* why people come through, but it was something she needed to deal with and learn from on her own. Even though I've said this over and over, it's worth repeating: those on the Other Side can't interfere with the karmic lessons we're here to learn. However, they can gently guide us, send us inspiration, let us know they're here to support us, and above all, confirm that they still love us.

Over the years, some remarkable messages have come through, many which have brought entire audiences to tears. I'd like to share a few of these stories with you. Some illustrate how a message is unexpectedly received, even from someone those on this side weren't expecting at all. Other stories show how a piece of information within a message can change someone's life forever. The following story is of a young man, and how he made sure his friend received an unexpected message from him to let her know he was alive and well in the Spirit World. It's one of those special communications that I still remember to this day. It not only touched the recipient, but everyone else in the room. With all messages, the information comes *through* me, and then I deliver it just like a postman delivers the mail! I'll never forget this one special occasion.

### A Room with a View

As I was getting ready one Saturday morning for a mediumship demonstration in Toronto, I knew there would be close to 1,000 people in the audience, all anxiously waiting to see if a loved one or friend would come through specifically for them. I was just getting dressed when the image of the fairy-tale character Snow White popped into my head. Even when I get a somewhat bizarre image such as this, I've trained myself to ask: "Are these my thoughts and impressions or maybe something I've seen recently on TV, or is it someone trying to get my attention from the Spirit World?"

Nowadays, it takes a strong spirit to get my attention before I've gone through my little ritual of opening myself up, which I do onstage so that the audience can witness what's happening. I open up my consciousness by raising my own vibrations. It takes a few minutes, and that's usually when spirits draw close, so when one gets through before I've opened up, then I know something's up!

In this case, this particular spirit made quite an impression, and I knew I couldn't ignore it. As bizarre as this might sound, what I actually saw in my mind was Snow White being carried in her crystal coffin on the shoulders of the seven dwarfs. Well, just about everyone knows the story of Snow White, who bit into a poisoned apple given to her by the evil queen. The dwarfs thought she was dead until a handsome prince saved the day by awakening her. According to the fairy tale, one day a young prince came to the dwarfs' house wanting shelter. When he saw Snow White lying there in a glass coffin, he begged the dwarfs to sell him the coffin with the dead Snow White, but they said no. He told them he couldn't live without being able to see her, and would honor and cherish her. Eventually, the dwarfs took pity on him and gave him her coffin.

I knew that this thought of Snow White and the crystal coffin was not mine. I certainly hadn't just read a book of fairy tales, and Snow White and the seven dwarfs had no significance in my life. As I buttoned up my shirt, I knew that a spirit was desperately trying to grab my attention, and was planting this unusual impression into my mind.

"John, five minutes!" I heard. The image of Snow White got automatically and subconsciously filed away. I tried to get ready, but another equally strange image started to form in my mind's eye. I saw the image of the old metal diving helmet used in the days before modern scuba equipment. Having dived many times myself, I knew these helmets were made of brass or copper, and were designed to encase the whole head with a small window. Once again, this single thought had appeared out of nowhere, although I knew these particular helmets had nothing to do with me.

Usually impressions like these — whether I'm seeing, hearing, or feeling them — tend to come to me while I'm onstage, usually after I've gone through my introduction describing how I work as a medium. On these rare occasions when it happens before an event, I know that someone is trying to jump the line! In the last few minutes before I went on, I filed the second impression away, too. As I left the room to head down to the waiting car, I reached out with my own thoughts and simply said to whoever was doing this, "See you at the event!" If the spirit was going to get a message to someone in the audience, then he or she was going to have to impress me again with these thoughts during the demonstration.

Arriving at the venue, I was taken to the side of the stage to get ready to go on. With all the seats taken, there was even a crowd standing at the back of the auditorium. I got the signal that the event was about to start and waited for the usual introduction and welcoming applause. I ran up the steps and onto the stage.

I launched straight into my standard introduction. It's very important for everyone (especially those who've never seen a medium work) to understand how I work, what they can expect, and how the afternoon will run. Usually it's when I give this speech that spirits start gathering around me. Sometimes it gets pretty crowded on that stage, and I can feel them jostling for a prime position to begin their communication. I can't and probably never will be able to totally describe the sensation. It's just that I'm aware that I'm no longer alone on the stage, but rather, it's filled with spirits anxiously waiting for me to begin. This day was no exception.

The messages and validations began to flow, one after the other, bringing healing and possibly closure to those who were lucky enough to receive the messages. As I've said previously in this chapter, I don't choose the spirits — they choose me. I stopped for a moment in between messages, and the impressions I'd received earlier about Snow White and the diving helmet popped back into my mind as clear as day. They almost merged together, more like one image. The spirit who had sent those messages was back!

In a split second, I knew what I was about to say. I could feel the excitement in my body as my energy raced in anticipation. At times like this, it's as if I'm seeing an entire movie in that moment, which enables me to interpret the image that much quicker. When I receive impressions with such clarity, whether they're just symbols or a full-blown image, it makes the saying "A picture is worth a thousand words" completely valid. By now, I was pacing back and forth across the stage frantically. I could feel the spirit guiding me, almost directing me to a certain section in the audience. I couldn't wait any longer and just started in.

"Ladies and gentlemen, you know that often I receive things, and I just have to give you what I'm getting." I paused long enough to breathe. "But I'm questioning this one! It's certainly different. Okay, here goes." I pointed to the area that I was drawn to and asked, "Does anyone in this section understand someone being buried in a coffin with a window?" Silence fell upon the audience.

Now in my own mind, that question didn't really make sense, but somehow I knew I was being guided to say just that. I honestly didn't think anyone was going to raise their hand. After all, who has a coffin with a window? I'd never heard of such a thing. Nothing surprises me anymore, though, and sure enough, an attractive middle-aged woman raised her hand. *Thank God!* I thought, peering toward the very back of the auditorium. I spoke directly to her.

"So let me get this right. You understand someone buried in a coffin with a window?!"

"Yes, John, I do," she replied with a calm, steady voice.

"Do you mind explaining this to me, because I've never heard of anything like this before, and this is a first for me, receiving information like this."

"Well, you see, John, it wasn't *really* a coffin. It was actually an urn. I'm a glassblower by trade, and a few years ago a very close friend of mine, Steven, passed away." She realized that everyone had turned around to look at her before she launched in again: "I wanted to do something special for him and his family. He was cremated, and I thought it would be a great gift for them if I could create a handblown-glass urn for his ashes. Here's the funny thing though, John: as I was blowing the glass, I decided to create a clear bubble on the outside of the urn so Steven would always have light and be able to see out through the bubble."

Anyone who's seen me work knows that I incorporate humor into my demonstrations, just to keep everything grounded and balanced and to raise the vibrations and energy, so I jokingly said to her, "So it's a room with a view, then, right?"

At that moment, the whole audience including myself felt shivers go up our spines, which also led right to everyone's heart. Everyone was touched by the message. Now I understood why Steven had come through earlier (the woman had confirmed his name before he'd had a chance to tell me) and shown me a crystal coffin followed by the metal diving helmet. Initially I thought it had been two separate spirits, not realizing that it was to be one combined impression. Crystal coffin meaning "burial," and the diving helmet with a window on the front so the diver could look out. The puzzle was complete after the woman's explanation.

Oftentimes a spirit has to use what's in my mind, searching for a reference that can be applied to the message, picking from my own internal database (to use a modern-technology term), as well as drawing from my own experiences and memories. They really know how to get me to say what I'm supposed to. It's almost like a game of psychic charades, but it works. Steven went on with the message, telling the woman just how grateful he was that she was in his life, and how touched he was by the special present she'd made for him.

"He's also telling me that you blow glass for children's charities, donating all the money to them," I went on.

She said with happy tears in her eyes, "Yes, he's quite right. This is something I've been doing for years, and I'll continue to do."

"Well, he says that your work doesn't go unnoticed, and that even the Spirit World is aware of your kind heart and generosity." I was acutely aware of how proud Steven was of this beautiful woman.

"He wants you to know that he'll check in on you, and he's encouraging you to keep up the good work. Oh, he's telling me that you must remember to be good to yourself in the process."

As I felt Steven's energy start to pull away, I wanted to tell her one more thing: "I have to applaud Steven for getting my attention in such a special way. He must be quite a persistent character, as he was pretty determined to make sure you received this message this afternoon."

Before the woman sat down, she looked at me and smiled. "Thank you, John, so much for that. I'm happy to be here, but wasn't really expecting a message."

All I could say in return as the audience members were giving her tissues to wipe away her tears was, "He did most of the work!" I felt the link disappear as fast as he'd arrived earlier, and Steven was gone, but he'd said exactly what he'd come to say. The applause said it all — everyone was touched. Even those who didn't receive a message that afternoon left with a sense of healing, knowing that their loved ones were still with them.

### *Return to Sender*

Not only am I constantly immersed in some book as part of my ongoing study of psychic mediumship, but I like to impart as much information as possible as a way of educating people. As I've already said, I like to begin each major demonstration with a little talk and some history, and usually I take an assortment of questions from the audience. One of the most important parts of the preliminary stage setting, as I call it, is some of the do's and don'ts, as well as some of the basic facts of just how this extraordinary form of communication works. Anyone who's seen my demonstrations will know that one of my signature openings is, "How many of you . . . ?" which is usually followed by a question related to the level of their experience or awareness. I always stress that anyone can come through with a message. Often, I get the audience warmed up by injecting a little humor, as laughter is a great way of raising the energy. I even let them know this by saying, "You know, my friends, I never, never, never embarrass you . . . they do! This is where all your stuff might come out, your habits, moods, or even one of your little quirks."

I can usually tell those who call out to their loved ones in their minds or to a specific person on the Other-Side. They're the ones who ask, and quite often demand, that spirits come through with a message for them. If I identify someone who's approaching the process in this way, I usually educate them quickly. Some people will even bring some object to the event, and I can almost imagine them saying to their friends in the lobby, "If he mentions this, then I'll know it's real." Some of these people even have code names or pet names that they want to hear me say to validate the message. I truly sense and understand their desperation, and as I've said previously, I never know who is going to come through.

There are times when someone may hear from an unrelated spirit whom the person knows, such as a friend or co-worker. When this occurs, it often prompts the typical question, "Why does that happen?" Say a mom wants to come through for her daughter, who's not at the event, but there's someone in the audience who works with the daughter. It's quite likely that the mom will use that person in the audience to get a message to her daughter. The person in the audience becomes the medium by delivering the message. Spirits know that they can reach out to you, and all being well, you'll deliver what was said.

So in my opening talk, I tell people, "Think beyond your family — because you never know who might show up. Spirits know what they're doing." I go on to explain that they might even hear from someone they really *don't* want to hear from. I have no control over it. This, in fact, happened in southern New England one evening, and I hope that those people learned a valuable lesson. As usual, I was in full swing, delivering messages, and this was the next link I got:

"I have a man here who so wants to come through. I'm walking over to the front row and over here to the right," I pointed almost directly into the audience. I knew where I was going with this one.

"It feels like someone's husband, and he's giving me the name Francis." I hardly stopped. I was so sure about the link; it was a strong one this time. I could see a woman and a young man talking back and forth to each other, not really paying attention to me. She was shaking her head and mouthing the word "No!" back at him. I really felt drawn to them, so I just carried on.

"Excuse me, hello . . . I have a man named Francis coming through, and he feels like your husband. Would you understand that?"

Finally, she looked up and stared right at me with a sense of surprise and irritation all over her face and said bluntly, "Yeah, *ex*-husband! His name was Francis, but we called him Frank."

I tried to maintain my composure for a split second, not wishing to respond to her rather agitated state. "Well, he's telling me that the young man who's sitting right beside you is your son . . . correct?"

"Yeah, that's right!" was her somewhat clipped response. I could feel the wall she was building between us. I've learned from years of doing this work that there's always a good explanation when someone is so upset or doesn't want to receive a message. There's always a reason, even if it's buried deep in the past. In this case, I could see that she was annoyed, but still I hadn't figured out why, so I persisted.

"So, Frank has a message for you." But before I'd barely finished the statement, she fired back with a tone of utter resentment.

"Well! Then I've got one for him!"

I was starting to lose a little patience now, and took a deep breath to remain calm.

"I think we all know what that's likely to be, lady!" I said, hoping to prevent her from saying too much.

Everyone in the audience understood from her comments that she clearly did not want to hear from her ex-husband. I could tell that she'd come to the event hoping to hear from someone else. I don't give up without a fight, as Frank was desperately trying to get a message to her, and when I'm on that stage, it's my job to deliver it the best as I can. Yet no matter how I tried to deliver the message, she just turned away and didn't want to hear it. It was like a battle. Frank knew that she was in the audience with their son and was being unbelievably stubborn. But he clearly wasn't about to give up and was determined to try different ways to get his message to her. He wouldn't leave me alone.

Nevertheless, the woman simply refused the message, over and over. At this point, I could sense the audience's irritation, too. They were becoming annoyed with her, and I didn't want to waste valuable time, so I reluctantly decided to cut the cord and break the link. I felt bad for Frank, though, as it wasn't his fault. I moved on to the next message.

As always, after such a demonstration, I spend time signing books, answering a few personal questions, and even giving a hug when it's needed. This evening was no different. My agent was sitting next to me as I was signing books and talking to a woman who'd patiently waited in line. Something made me look down the line, and I noticed that Frank's wife and son were waiting to talk to me. She didn't look happy.

As I greeted her and shook her hand and then her son's, she told me, "I didn't want to hear from him! I wanted my mother!"

"Yes, I understand that, but as I explained at the start, I have no control over who comes through, and he did have a message for you."

"Well, I wanted my mother," she repeated again. With that, she simply walked away with her son. My heart went out to her. Obviously, she wasn't in a place of forgiveness and had come to the event so desperately wanting to hear from her beloved mother, and certainly not her ex-husband. While you may be sensing the same frustration that many in the audience felt that night, since any message would have been a blessing for some, there's a point to this story that I want to share.

What she and most people didn't realize that night was just how much energy it took for Frank to come through, to lower his energy as I raised mine enough for the link to be created. I'd sensed just how much energy it had taken for Frank to make his presence known, as he'd guided me almost directly to his wife and son. With a crystal-clear voice he'd given me his name, and told me that he was her husband and the father to the boy, so they were left with no doubt who was trying to give them a message. That was a lot of work for both him and for me, and sadly, the woman just turned away, refusing to listen or even accept the message — a message she'll never hear.

What's really sad is that her husband was trying to come through with an apology about his abuse and his alcoholism; he was reaching out to her for forgiveness and also wanted to wish his son a happy birthday. I can understand that she may have endured a miserable life with him, but who are we to judge? It's impossible to tell who might have been right behind her husband, someone whom he might have helped come through for her. Yes, maybe even her mother! We'll never know, because she couldn't look past her own anger, so that message was just stamped: "Returned to Sender."

This happened many years ago, so I hope that Frank's ex-wife and son have now found some type of healing and have been able to forgive Frank for his faults. If you're asking why I've told this story, it's really for those of you who need to deal with something similar in your own lives, or who may be struggling or blaming others or even yourselves. Is there someone here, living, who needs forgiveness? Or if they're on the Other-Side, they still might need your forgiveness. It's never too late to say it, ever. Therefore, I hope Frank's story will help you appreciate how a message can come through, and more important, what you can expect. All I ask is that you give the spirits a chance and allow them to do what they have to. They're in control — not me. I'm simply the spirit whisperer.

### Pizza Girl

We all need a break once in a while — to meet up with friends, to swap the latest news, to laugh, and to just get away from our daily working lives — in other words, to just be. Growing up half Italian and eating my mom's cooking, I now find that I'm always up for a good pizza! One night I'd planned to meet a group of friends, and we found the perfect spot. We'd heard about a place to go for the best pizza in town. Miraculously, we all managed to arrive on time and squeezed into a booth, eager to hear what everyone had been up to recently. The aromatic, spicy smells of pizza made us all even hungrier, and each time the ovens were opened to slide out another freshly baked one, I think we all drooled with expectation! A lovely waitress must have seen our looks, so she came up to take our order for food and beverages.

As she returned with a full tray of drinks, she stared directly at me as if she'd seen me before. I could see the telltale look of curiosity all over her face. She looked at me once again and casually said, "You look very familiar. Have you been in here before?"

"No, this is our first time. We're just looking forward to our pizzas," I said, hoping she'd get the message that we were rather hungry.

Undeterred, she went on. "I'm sorry, but you look so familiar to me."

My friends stopped talking as they became aware of what was going on. This often happened when we were out together. One of them looked at me with that all-knowing smile and muttered to herself, "Here we go again!"

Would the waitress figure out who I was? So as to not keep her guessing any longer, and to keep our group from dying of thirst, I decided to put her out of her misery and ask her if she ever went to a certain bookstore in that area.

"Yes, every once in a while, I do go there when I have time," she replied.

"Have you ever seen a medium there named John?"

"Um . . . oh my God! Oh my God! It's you!" she screamed as she began to rattle the remaining glasses that were still delicately balanced on her tray.

"Why don't you put down the drinks before we're wearing them." I smiled.

"I'm so embarrassed. Oh, please forgive me," she went on, and I thought at that, she would turn around to continue serving, but no, she went on.

"I have to talk to you about what happened when you gave me a message some years ago. Would you mind if I come back and talk to you after you're finished eating?"

I was not quite sure why I said yes, bearing in mind I was out with friends, but something inside me just told me to say, "Of course, I would be happy to."

I've given thousands and thousands of messages over the years, and I'd love to be able to say that I can remember every one, but it's totally impossible. People take those messages back to their families, and I believe that in many cases, they help with the process of healing from their loss. It's rare, unless someone writes to me, that I ever get to hear what happens when these people take a message home and how the ripple effect of love can start. After my friends and I enjoyed our meal, paid our bills, took our leftovers, and said our good-byes, I found my way to the kitchen to see the rather nervous waitress, Sandy.

She thanked me profusely for taking the time to speak with her. I could tell that she was anxious to tell me her story. I perched on a stool and encouraged her to talk.

"John, some years ago, as you now know, I was at the bookstore here, but I had no idea you were going to be speaking that evening. If I'm really honest, John, I didn't know who you were, or more to the point, *what* you were."

I told her that I was not that well known in those days and that I wasn't offended at all. I even told her that if I had my way now, I would prefer not being recognized. She was obviously a woman with a mission and continued.

"John, there were only about 35 people there that night due to the limited space, and I was lucky enough to get one of the few remaining tickets. As I sat there watching you give messages, I stopped for a moment to think of who I knew in the Spirit World — grandparents, aunts, uncles, and of course, my father, who left us to marry another woman and begin a new family with her. I still remember what happened as if it were yesterday." She'd gotten my attention now, as I was eager to see where this was going.

"You were just about out of time when you came to me. I was sitting in the very last row. You started by pointing straight at me and calmly said, 'I want to come to the young woman in the back row. Yes, you, the lady in front of the bookshelf there. I have your father here, and he's asking for forgiveness from you. Do you understand that?'

"I was so shocked, John, I didn't know what to say except a simple yes," she said with a slight wobble in her voice. I could tell this was an important story for her.

"You described my dad's personality, what he did for work, and how he never stopped loving me. Validation upon validation came flying out of you! I hardly had time to take it all in. John, although you probably don't remember this, you were finishing with the message and you said to me, 'Just one more thing.' I didn't understand it then, but you said, 'Your dad wants me to tell you he just met up with Charlie!'

"I could understand everything in the message except for that last comment, John. I went home that night thankful for the opportunity you'd given me to hear from my dad, but I couldn't let go of the last message about Charlie. I went through all the people and friends in his life, but I couldn't recall the name Charlie. I tried to let it go, but for weeks, that evening kept popping up in my mind. It would come up just as I was trying to sleep, or while I was working. I had to find out one way or another who this person was that my father mentioned." She got up and poured us both a glass of water before carrying on.

"Finally, I had to give in, and decided that the only way I would ever sort out this mystery was to call my half-brother and see if he could identify this Charlie who my dad had met up with. Well, you see, John, my father had a son after he'd left my family. I haven't spoken to him — my half-brother — in many years, nor did I ever plan to or even want to. I figured that was my dad's new family, and for my own reasons, I didn't want to have anything to do with them. When I called, my half-brother was really surprised that I'd phoned him out of the blue like that. We exchanged some polite hellos and had a few awkward moments as we somewhat superficially caught up. I had to get to the point of my call, and finally told him the reason I was contacting him. I wasn't at all sure how he was reacting to this information about a message from a medium, or even how he felt about life after death."

I was perched on the edge of my stool listening to her. "Go on, Sandy, finish the story."

"I told him I went to see you at this bookstore and that you gave me several validations about our dad, enough to know it was him."

She continued telling me how she'd asked about the mysterious Charlie. Her half-brother had told her that he was open to the whole concept of life after death and was not remotely surprised that their dad had mentioned Charlie.

She looked deeply into my eyes. "Anxiously, I asked, 'Well, who is he, then?' He told me that our dad and Charlie had worked together for many years. It was Charlie who'd driven him to work every day. He went on to tell me that Charlie had recently passed and explained how he and our father had grown really close after spending so much time together."

At that moment, I realized that this whole experience of her dad simply mentioning a dear friend had a more profound effect. He'd wanted to bring his extended family closer after many years of discomfort and turmoil. I think he'd gotten his wish. Sandy finished up telling me how she's now much closer to her half-brother and his two daughters, whom she adores. She said that she'd become their favorite aunt!

"You know, John, they're like angels who have been sent to me, and I love them so much. Imagine, I might never have known my brother better or his children if I hadn't been at that bookstore that evening."

I made a little mental note to myself that as she ended the story, she'd dropped the "half" and was referring to him as her brother.

I thanked her for this heartfelt story, and I often tell it onstage to show people how healing can happen long after someone has left this world. We both hugged as we were saying good-bye, and she looked at me with a smile. "John, the next pizza is on me. I owe you one!"

All I could say back was, "I'm just doing my job."

I know I've said it before, but I will say it again: I'm constantly amazed by how those on the Other-Side can help us here, and that they continue to love us and watch over us. I'm sure Sandy's father is quite happy about his family reunion, and somehow I believe he knew it would happen all along. All Sandy needed was a gentle nudge.

# CHAPTER 8

## LOVE NEVER DIES

For the majority of us, from an early age we learn that when we grow up, it's quite likely that we'll meet the person we're supposed to spend the rest of our life with. We're taught that there's *someone* for *everyone*. As we grow up and develop our own individuality, we give our hearts to each other as we search for that everlasting love. Some of us are fortunate enough to find that special person; we stand in front of God and family and pledge our undying love and commitment to each other, for richer or poorer, in sickness and in health, and so on.

In those wonderful early days, where love has no boundaries, we plan on growing old together as we take on the challenges of life with courage and strength, standing side by side. No one is ever ready when that special person, the one we thought would be with us each and every day, is no longer there. I know that in our modern society, not every couple remains together in a bond of unity and love, but for many it is just so.

How you deal with this type of loss naturally depends on the circumstances. If the death of your life partner is sudden, with little or no warning, then there's the horrible feeling that you never got time to say good-bye. Whereas in the situation of a long-term illness, there's often time to express what's in your heart, but the downside is that you more than likely have to watch your loved one suffer. In this situation, there's often a feeling of guilt, coupled with relief that your life partner has finally passed and isn't in pain anymore. Please know that these types of emotions are totally normal — *no one* wants to see anyone they care for suffer, especially when there's dignity and a sense of independence involved, and they always want you to remember them as they were: healthy, strong, and vibrant, because in reality that is how they are on the Other-Side.

Of course, given the work I do, I deal with both types of loss, and all too often, people sit opposite me with the usual list of unanswered questions, such as: *Did I say enough? Did I do enough? Do they know how much I love them? Can I fulfill the dreams we had on my own now? Am I strong enough to get through this?* People tell me about their loneliness and their aching hearts, saying it's all they can bear.

As the reality of becoming an "I" rather than "we" dawns, practicalities of managing the finances, bringing up the children or even grandchildren, and making important decisions are some of the immediate challenges. Then, coupled with the practical stressors, there's often anger at the universe or a loss of faith in a Higher Power. Again, these are natural responses to grief, and it doesn't matter how old you are or how long you've been with your partner; it's perfectly okay to feel such strong emotions.

I want to include a few stories that I hope will offer some comfort and solace for those who are experiencing such a loss. These accounts will help you know that love really is eternal, a force that can never, ever be broken.

### Edward and Ellen

I was standing outside an 18th-century farmhouse on the outskirts of Portsmouth, New Hampshire, within which is a holistic-treatment clinic. Given my simple taste in architecture, I love the warm colors of the handmade stone walls and often finish my coffee in the garden, with its flowering shrubs that give off a beautiful scent when the breeze swirls. It's a unique place where I book a consulting room for seeing families who've lost loved ones — a place of beauty that has become my sanctuary.

This afternoon was no different, as I took my last sip of iced coffee and prepared for the next group, who were arriving for what they hoped would be a reunion with the Spirit World — a chance for them to connect with people they'd lost. Some of the group came with the hopes of getting a message from loved ones who had suffered, so they'd had time to prepare; while others were coming to hopefully say their good-byes, as their loss had been all too sudden.

I could see cars pulling up. I glanced over toward the parking lot and noticed an older gentleman getting out of his car. He was on his own. As he walked past me with a somber look on his face, we said a brief hello, I introduced myself, and he told me his name was Ed as he quickly went inside to join the others. He didn't realize that at that very moment, I felt his wife walking right behind him. It's more common in our society that the husband is the one to pass on first, leaving his wife a widow. Women seem to stay here longer to be with their families, whereas men somehow have a tougher time being on their own.

That afternoon, I knew that Ed was in for a big surprise, as he was about to hear from his loving wife of 45 years. She was already connecting with me, eager to tell him to be strong. I could see that she wanted him to live out the rest of his life in happiness and to spend as much time with the family as possible. I felt her love directed toward him. I also felt this was going to be a good group.

There was the usual nervous chatter as people sat down. I can always feel the sense of anxiety, and the excitement often created from the unexpected. After all, I don't really know what is going to happen at these groups. Ed took his seat with that weariness that often stems from sadness. Little did he know that everything was about to dramatically change!

The afternoon followed the usual format, with me bringing through messages for the people in the group. I was in midsentence with one message when I looked up at Ed and saw tears in his eyes as he hung his head. This was his first experience sitting with a medium, and clearly, he was feeling his love for his wife and how much he was missing her. As I finished the message, I knew it was his turn. His wife, who'd been patiently waiting, immediately drew close.

"Ed, I want to come to you now. When you walked in, your beloved wife was walking right behind you. Am I correct in saying you've lost your wife?"

Ed looked up at the faces in the group and then at me as he nodded his head. He was visibly trembling with emotion. I could feel his pain and went on gently. "Well, Ed, your wife is here right next to me, and she's telling me that you brought your wedding ring with you this afternoon, and it's in your pocket."

Everyone in the group was being so supportive, sending their love to Ed at that moment. His face said it all as he reached inside his pocket and pulled out the ring his bride had given him on their wedding day so many years ago. He told me later, as he was leaving, that he'd brought it to see how good I was, and to see if I'd mention the ring in the reading. I remember telling him that it was Ellen, not me, who was good, and that she'd seen him put the ring in his pocket before he left the house. I told him that she'd heard his thoughts.

I could feel Ellen's deep and unwavering love for Ed, and knew that she could sense just how much he was struggling without her by his side, almost as if a piece of him had been cut away when she passed. "Ed, she's telling me how she used to massage your head every evening. She's now showing me a picture of Lucille Ball. What's that all about?"

Ed's face broke out into a smile that ignited the light within him. "I loved my head massages, and she's showing you that because she was also a petite, gorgeous redhead!"

"She must have been quite a looker, Ed, because she's now showing me an image of the famous actress Rita Hayworth!" I could see Ed gaze off into the distance, as if the image of Ellen was touching his soul again. He told me that he never noticed until recently that in the corner of his wife's vanity mirror was a small black-and-white photograph of Rita Hayworth, tucked inside the upper frame of the mirror.

"She's telling me, Ed, how much she loves you, but she *had* to leave. She's telling me, Ed, that she was ready to go. She's acknowledging how you wiped the tear away from her face the moment she passed. Her cancer is all gone now, Ed. She's no longer suffering."

As the tears rolled down his face, another member of the group reached out and handed him a tissue. I knew he and Ellen had been childhood sweethearts, and how the two had been totally inseparable. I confirmed that I knew they had been married when they were only 18 and that there had been no one else in their whole lives, just each other. I only know one couple in my life that has been married since they were at school together. They're still inseparable to this day, knowing no other partner than the other. I went on talking to Ed.

"You two were joined at the hip."

"John, it's what I always say when I talk about the love of my life," he replied.

I could feel Ed's loneliness and his ongoing struggle to be strong for himself as well as his family. Ellen wanted to make sure that he knew she was still there to support him, but he needed to finish his life until they met again.

"Ed, your redhead is showing me how you stroked her hair at the funeral parlor and the pain you were going through on that sad day. She wants you to be happy, Ed, and to be here for the children, as they need you very much."

"I know, John. I'm trying to be strong."

"I know you are, Ed, and your wife wants me to acknowledge Joyce and Lois. Do you understand that?" Ellen gave me the two names with such clarity that I was left with no doubt.

"Yes, yes, they're my wife's dearest friends," he said with a face that was alert and full of life. What a change from the sad face that had walked in earlier that afternoon.

I went on: "Well, Ed, please tell them your wife says hello and that this is a special shout-out to them."

Ed smiled, knowing that Ellen's friends would be thrilled to hear from her when he got home. He would phone them right away, as they knew he was coming to the group. Ellen made it quite clear to me that she hadn't finished and was still talking to him, even though it was my voice.

"Ed, she's telling me that she saw you at a birthday party in July. Is that correct?"

"Yes, John, that's true, I did go to a party, but I left early because it was so hard to be there without my Ellen."

"I understand, Ed. You know, some people take much longer to stop saying 'we' before they're ready to just use the word 'I.'"

"So true, John, so true," he replied, as though he was being given permission to start saying "I" in his own life. I was privileged to be giving him this message, as the bond between them was beautiful, full of love and compassion.

"She still is and always was so proud of you, Ed. She's telling me how proud she was of what you did. I feel as if you *served* your country in somewhat of a legal capacity. Am I getting that right, Ed?"

Ed began to smile even more as he said, "I was a sergeant in the Army, and now I'm a part-time police officer!"

"She's so proud, Ed, so proud of you and the people you help. She so wants you to know she *really* is there with you. She's showing me the grandfather clock in your home, and that the pendulum no longer swings. Ed, she's telling me that she's going to make that clock chime, so when it does, you'll know it's her saying hello, okay?"

Everyone in the group looked at Ed, many of them touched by the gentleness of Ellen's spirit and the love being directed his way. Ed validated that, in fact, they did have an antique grandfather clock in their home, and the pendulum hadn't moved for years. He smiled as he told me that he hadn't gotten around to having it fixed yet.

I could feel Ellen begin to pull back as another spirit was stepping forward. I'm sure that with his wife's help, we gave Ed some strength that special afternoon, knowing that his wife of 45 years still holds her husband and family close to her soul; and that all their memories, sorrows, and joys go with us when we pass, for they are truly what make us unique . . . and forever eternal.

When I started to write this book, I left Ed a voice mail asking him if he was comfortable with me using his story for this book. He called back to give his approval and told me that the previous morning, the chimes on the grandfather clock had tinkled softly six times in a row. It was as if Ellen's fingers were caressing the chimes to make good on her promise that she would give him a sign. Ed was totally elated, as he had doubted whether such a thing was really possible.

### Remembering the Swans

When we lose a partner or another loved one, some of the signs we might receive can be extraordinary and quite unique. Often, they remind us of that special someone who has passed over and how we're always connected; yet more important, they also remind us that death doesn't separate us. Those signs could be a sudden memory, a symbol, or a particular saying that was unique to the person. I'll talk later in this chapter about ADCs (the After Death Communications I mentioned earlier), which are signs from your loved ones to let you know their souls are, in fact, still alive.

Some people have a certain affinity for butterflies, flowers, certain smells, songs, or even in the case of the next story, swans. It was featured in my first book, *Born Knowing*, and the story touched many readers, as well as myself. I want to share it again with you and hope that it offers some comfort if you've lost someone. This story just proves that people really never change, and that the love that was given to you here continues to grow forever.

I immediately liked Ruth, an attractive, soft-spoken woman in her 60s who worked as a real-estate agent in Florida. She had beautiful cornflower blue eyes and a warm smile, but I could see and feel that she was clearly in pain. She started talking as she was sitting down.

"I just wanted to see if there was something to this medium work," she said. "I need some answers, and I'm not sure where else to turn. So my favorite cousin suggested you as a possible solution."

From her opening statement, I couldn't tell whether she'd never been to a medium or if she was a bit skeptical. I was about to say something when she made a little confession. "John, I'm not what you'd call a total believer," she said, looking down at her toes as if such a statement might offend me.

I just smiled at her and said, "Ruth, many people come to see me, and I'm sure that most of them are thinking the same thing. I think that *everyone* should be a little skeptical. After all, it's healthier that way. I admire the fact that you were brave enough to say it." I touched her hand and gently said, "Let's just see what happens."

Ruth's self-confidence seemed to spike a bit when she saw that I wasn't judging her belief system, but I had no idea that the messages were about to turn those beliefs around.

"Ruth, I feel as if I have a husband figure here. Do you have a husband who's crossed?"

"Why, yes!" she said. "My Eddie!"

"Ruth, I know a lot of men don't like to wear rings, but I feel as if Eddie liked to wear two. In fact, he's showing me two rings on one hand. Is that right?"

Ruth began to weep and smile at the same time. She told me that Eddie had passed away six months ago, and he was buried with his two favorite rings. "He wore his late father's wedding ring on one finger, and our wedding ring on another," she said.

My hand went up to my chest, where I felt some pain as I said, "What's with his heart?"

Ruth went on to tell me that Eddie had passed from a massive heart attack.

"There's a lot of love coming through here, Ruth. This man doted on you. He had a strong personality, too. Correct?"

Ruth nodded.

"He's sending you his strength because he knows that you keep thinking he's far away. Now he's showing me pages and pages of lists. Do you understand this?"

"He always made lists to get everything accomplished. Everyone loved him because he was always in control and got the job done," Ruth said.

"I see him in a uniform."

"Eddie was an officer in the Navy during World War II. Later on, he took that strong personality of his and became a very successful businessman," she said, smiling with pride. "He was at the top of his field, a mechanical engineer. He even owned his own company."

"He's talking about how he almost passed twice and how he fooled the doctors," I said. "He knows you were there for him, and he thanks you so much for helping him when he was sick. He wants you to know that he's in excellent health now; and he's no longer attached to his old, failing body. He's telling me there were multiple things wrong with him. Why am I being drawn to my back?"

"He had a kidney transplant," Ruth said.

"He was a real trouper — they had to drag him into the Spirit World." I touched my heart again. "What's with the feeling in my chest? I'm seeing stitches there. Did they operate on his heart as well?"

"Yes, he also had a heart transplant," Ruth replied, hugging herself.

"Your love gave him a lot of the strength that kept him here during many amazing struggles. In fact, his love for you willed him to stay on this earth much longer." At this point, I was also getting emotional, which I usually don't do — but this was such a touching and amazing story. I cleared my throat and continued. "Ruth, why does he keep saying to me over and over that he wants you to . . . remember the swans? What does that mean?"

Ruth suddenly turned white, as though I'd said something totally unexpected. I watched as she took a few long, deep breaths before she found the composure to carry on.

"What's that, Ruth? What does it mean?" I gently prodded her, knowing it must be something very personal and very significant.

Finally, she managed to speak. "We used to sit on our favorite bench on our property and look at these magnificent white swans that lived on the lake. One afternoon Eddie turned to me and said, 'Ruth, you see those swans out there? Swans mate forever — just like us, Ruthie. We're a pair of old swans.'"

I could see Ruth reliving this happy memory. Suddenly, it was as if she was back with Eddie on their bench at dusk, holding hands and looking out on a scene that would make an artist want to pick up a paintbrush.

When I felt that Ruth was ready to continue, I carried on. "Now Eddie's asking you, 'Why aren't you out with your friends? Just because I'm not there doesn't mean you have to stay in the house.'"

"I have a hard time going out because he's not with me," she confirmed, knowing that it was a delicate point.

"But he *is* with you, Ruth," I said. "Eddie wants you to continue to have those dinner parties. He wants you to remember the fun times you had together, but he so much wants you to surround yourself with your friends so that you can have good times in the future." I paused for a moment. "I see roses — I usually don't give flowers in a sitting, as they're so common. Everybody gets flowers, but Eddie's handing you *a lot* of roses."

Ruth smiled. "He used to give me flowers all the time, John. On my 60th birthday, he took me to our favorite restaurant. Before a special cake was delivered for dessert, Eddie had the waiter bring over 60 long-stemmed roses."

"Well, he's adding a few more to the bunch," I said. "I hope this helps you believe — not just for today, but forever."

She looked directly into my eyes before she said, "John, I'll try to find it in me to be with my friends because I do miss them terribly. It'll be easier now that I know Eddie's with me."

With that, she smiled, thinking that her session was over, but I had one more thing to tell her. "Ruth, do you understand this? Now Eddie's talking about you gazing out the window every morning into your garden. He's saying there's something else there besides just flowers."

Ruth was beaming now. "Before Eddie got sick, he bought me two beautiful ceramic swans to put in my garden," she said. "I still have those swans, even though they're very old and weathered now. Every morning I look at them the first moment I open my eyes . . . and yes, I'll remember the swans. Forever."

This has to be one of the most touching readings I've ever given anyone, and it gives me great pleasure to include it again here. It's one of those stories that illustrates the healing qualities and unending power of love.

## I'll Always Love You

This is a story I'll always remember. It's just one of those amazing messages that few mediums ever forget. I've been giving public demonstrations for many years; and over time, the audiences have grown, yet it really doesn't matter whether there are 10 or 10,000. Sometimes, there's one special message that seems to just stand out above the rest. Somehow, certain messages touch people in a profound way, and even if during the demonstration they don't get anything personally, one particular message resonates with them and they take home what they heard and share it with others. One single message for one person can affect many. Strangely enough, they often come right at the end of the demonstration, just when I think my link with the Spirit World is fading; it's as though that one last spirit leaps forward to grab my attention and won't go until I've made the connection. I have to keep my energy raised that much longer to keep the link open.

On this particular evening on my home turf in Boston, it was a sold-out audience, and I was excited to be back. I'd even bought a new suit with a brilliantly colored shirt. My manager had everything organized, and we dressed the stage in black velvet with purple lighting, which looked awesome. There was a single stool onstage and an antique easel with a huge print of my latest book at that time, *Psychic Navigator.* We'd laid out more than a dozen beautiful white roses across the front of the stage, all individually wrapped with white ribbons. It was my own way of finishing a message, as my runners would give each recipient one of the roses. It's become my personal trademark, and people love taking them home to remember and honor the message they've just received.

It had been a brilliant evening, and as always, I had no idea how much time I had left. I glanced down at the front of the stage and noticed there was just one rose left. At the same time, I got the signal saying I needed to stop. I knew as tired as I was that I had to squeeze in just one more! Immediately, I was drawn to the back of the auditorium. In the far corner, I couldn't see a thing, as the lighting was too dim. I knew I was being guided to one specific area. In my mind, I kept seeing things and feeling as if I were going down in a plane. It was a terrifying feeling, and I could sense the panic and fear throughout my entire body. I knew I had to ask, and so I pointed toward the far left-hand corner.

"Would someone understand a plane accident, like a crash or a plane falling from the sky, and someone passing on that plane? I feel that this is a message from a young man!" No one uttered a word, but everyone almost simultaneously turned to face the back of the auditorium.

When I get such a strong link, as this was, I feel as though I am reliving the whole experience that the spirit must have gone through. I knew he was reaching out with all his love to make a connection with a woman. I was sure she was at the back, sitting there in the darkness.

After the silence came this ever-so-soft voice. I could only hear her as she spoke from the darkness. It sounded as though she was a young woman.

"John, I understand the message of a plane going down," she almost whispered. A runner scrambled up the stairs and handed her a microphone.

"Would you understand that I have a male energy with me who keeps telling me over and over that he's so sorry?" I said. "I don't feel as though he's your father or an older male, but more your age, and I feel overwhelming love coming your way. He's quite calm and self-assured, but he's telling me it was impossible to get through on his cell phone."

At that, I felt the spirit's presence draw even closer. He clearly wanted my undivided attention. Well, he certainly had it now! I stepped forward slightly to get out of the glare of a spotlight, so I could now see the woman's face in the faint light. I saw how composed she was. I asked her to say her name.

"Amanda," she answered, and as she responded, I felt an upsurge of energy. This usually means I have the right person, as the link becomes even stronger and intensifies.

"He's telling me more, Amanda," I went on, "about the rock?" Well, that was enough. As she gasped, I knew I'd touched a nerve, but I had something important to tell her. It was coming in fast. I could tell that the spirit was so happy to be here, talking to Amanda. The only way I can describe the feeling is that it's like being on a computer when you download some software; but in my case it's a jumble of images, feelings, emotions, and words that miraculously get unscrambled as I speak. Knowing how I was going to deliver delicate information such as this was never easy.

"Amanda, he's telling me he didn't suffer, didn't feel a thing, that he was with other brave people . . . does this mean anything to you?" Before she had a chance to answer, I felt the jolt of the crash. I quivered and knew immediately that he'd been on the third plane that had gone down on September 11th. Of course, I'd been glued to the news for days at that time, and even though I knew the facts, he was showing me how some of the passengers had tried to overcome the terrorists. I gently explained that I knew how he'd died, but more important, how brave he'd been. She just nodded.

I had to compose myself for a second or two, and I could hear the whispers from the audience, most of whom had turned to face the back as they wanted to see this young woman receive her special message. This was without a doubt one of those readings that I knew we'd all remember for a long time to come.

"He's okay, you know that, but I'll say this, Amanda, he's quite insistent. He wants me to mention the rock again, as though this is something significant for you." I had no idea at that moment what sort of rock he was talking about. Then she spoke.

"Yes, John, the rock is special. My husband and I chose a special rock at a beach on Cape Cod, and every year on our wedding anniversary, we'd go and celebrate by sitting on this rock with a bottle of champagne." She stopped to catch her breath, before continuing, "Since September 11th, and every year without fail, I've gone back to *our* rock on my own. I've often felt his presence there with me, but never knew for sure. Over the years, I've started to realize that I have to move on." Before she could go on, her husband spoke again.

"Amanda, he's telling me that he *was* with you every year. He was there. He touched and caressed your hair when you were thinking about him as you looked over the sunrise on the ocean; and he knows how much you love and miss him, but he wants you to be happy. He knows about the new man in your life, and he wants you to be with him, to be happy and to let you know it's okay to love and laugh again. You so deserve it." The audience sat there in stunned silence, caught up in the tenderness of the message.

Amanda told me that, indeed, she had met someone special, but she felt so guilty moving on. She said that the message she'd just received was what she so needed to hear. The gentleman that she'd been seeing for some time had asked her numerous times for her hand in marriage, but she had been unable to answer him, constantly telling him she wasn't ready. Yet her heart so wanted to completely love again. She also told me that he was willing to wait until she was ready. I thought to myself, but didn't share it with the audience, what a lovely and strong man he sounded like, and that she really was meant to be with him.

"Finally, John, I can go home and tell him yes. I am ready now."

"Amanda, your husband is telling me how lucky he was to have you in his life, and all your memories together are exactly what he took with him when he passed, and that the last thoughts he had on that plane were of you and you only." I could just hear his last faint whisper to her as he stepped back, so I repeated it as a whisper to her: "I'll always love you."

The whole audience almost dissolved into tears because not only were they touched by this delicate message, but it brought back memories of that awful terrorist attack and the impact it had on the world. I watched as applause erupted, and people sitting in Amanda's area stood up and hugged her as my last white rose was handed to her.

I felt a sense of pure joy and happiness for Amanda. I was sure she'd be able to move on with her life. I knew she'd always hold a space in her heart and soul for her first husband, but with his blessing, she could continue to enjoy life to the fullest.

+·※·+

Through my work, I've discovered that many individuals find it hard to move on when they lose a spouse or a partner. While some people feel guilty moving on, others feel like they're cheating on the person who has passed. Still others feel they don't deserve to be happy and choose to go through the rest of their lives alone. Those on the Other-Side don't want us to linger in pain or to be alone. They know that as humans, we need to touch and to be touched, to hold and be held, and that above all, we're meant to love and be loved. There's never any judgment from them when it comes to affairs of the heart, and when you feel you cannot get out of bed because of your sadness, it is *they* who gently try to push you forward.

To cope with the loss of your life partner, the best advice I can give is that he or she wouldn't want you to suffer alone. I recommend that you talk to someone about your feelings, be it a close friend or a professional therapist. It doesn't help if you shut yourself off from those who were part of your life when you were a couple. Often, the spouse who is left on Earth feels as if he or she is not welcome in the old group, or feels guilty about socializing.

Yes, of course, it takes guts to go out alone and integrate back into the group, but you can do it. Often, you might find that your friends avoid the subject of your loss because they think it will be upsetting. Yet true healing comes from talking about how you miss your beloved partner. I always recommend that you try to include your loved ones who have passed in events, parties, or family gatherings. Toast them, talk about them, ask for a sign, and even take out pictures of them, particularly when they were happy. Let them know how much you still love them, because they feel it all.

In almost every reading, a loved one comes through to validate a certain event. It could be a wedding, a baby shower, a special vacation cruise, a birthday party, or simply a walk on the beach. Just because they're no longer in a body doesn't mean they're not enjoying being with their loved ones still.

There is work to do when you lose someone. You have to go through the bereavement process. Healing can only occur when you deal with your confusion, anger, and grief and know that you can stand on your own . . . with your loved one standing right beside you.

# CHAPTER 9

## SIGNS AND SYMBOLS: CALLING CARDS FROM HEAVEN

Memories of living in England, as you know from reading so far, are very special to me. It seems like a lifetime ago that I was walking the breathtaking grounds and the many halls of the Arthur Findlay College, which is nestled in the depths of the English countryside. The college, which I've affectionately nick-named my personal "Spirit Boot Camp," offers facilities unequaled anywhere in the world. It's a residential center where students can study Spiritualist philosophy, healing, and awareness and learn to develop their psychic and mediumship abilities. It's a place for like-minded people to discover their own unique spiritual talents. It's an amazing environment where you can discover who you are and in what direction you want to take your life. I always loved it there — not just for the education, but as a place where I was quite comfortable in knowing that I was not the *different* one anymore.

I don't think I ever realized as I was being groomed just how much my life would change after those intensive weeks of training. I was put through my paces, often with little time to think. The teachings were taken very seriously, and I was indoctrinated with a deep sense of integrity and commitment to the work. I remember one particular week I spent with about 80 other aspiring mediums, where we immersed ourselves for several days, learning about different signs and symbols and how to interpret them for future reference.

I found this to be a particularly fascinating part of the course, and the interpretations have become part of my methodology. We were encouraged to continue our training and to sit in a circle, so after each of the weeklong courses at the college, I'd return to Bristol feeling both exhilarated and drained at the same time. I then devoted every Tuesday evening to sitting in a mediumship development circle.

Although I knew even at that stage that I possessed something — some gift — and even though I wasn't able to quantify it then, I felt it deep within me. I knew, as I had since I'd been a child, that I was different, and that I was destined to do this work. Now, 17 years later, having taught many workshops myself, I realize that we all have the ability to link with Spirit in some way. For most people, the obstacle is often that they're totally unaware of, or have never contemplated communicating with, a loved one or a guide on the Other-Side.

My two-year circle training was probably my greatest preparation for developing and understanding how *my* mediumship worked, as I was taught many techniques showing me how to be aware when my guides and spirits were drawing close. These circles were highly disciplined, run by a strict code of ethics for those wanting to develop. I was blessed to be part of such a strong circle.

Using meditation as a technique, I was taught how to still my mind. This amazing process enables you to let go of the constraining influences of the outside world. When I mastered this silencing technique, I was able to make room for those on the Other-Side to merge with my own energy. By the same token, I had to learn to blend my energy with theirs. It was most definitely a two-way process. I was shown how to raise my consciousness and to reach out to them.

The experienced members of the circle helped me to heighten my senses and notice whether I was sensing, hearing, or seeing anything in my mind's eye. "John, just let yourself become fully aware of everything you're feeling, hearing, or seeing, and tell us what the spirits are trying to send to you," they would quietly repeat over and over. I would sit there week after week and attempt to interpret the signs and symbols. With each passing week, I found that it got easier to feel when I was receiving a message. This training certainly taught me that you can't rush this process, as it takes time and everyone will develop in their own way, in their own time, and yes, it takes . . . a lot of patience.

Often, I would experience a warm, comfortable feeling around my shoulders when the link opened. It signaled that I was about to forge a connection between this world and the next. I can only liken it to the feeling of someone wrapping a soft blanket around me. In the first few months of my development, it became my special *calling card.* Each time I felt this comforting blanket, I knew that my guides and potential spirits wanted to come through with a message. Some of the people in my development circle had their own calling cards when they were linking. I remember one of them saying she'd feel a breeze, whereas another woman saw colors, while one of the few other men there said that he felt a gentle hand on his shoulder.

Of course, everyone is different in how they feel or perceive people in the Spirit World when they're drawing close. After a while, when I opened myself up, I didn't need the rest of the group to confirm they were there. I began to trust and simply *know* that they were. Then one day I realized that I didn't even need to use my unique calling card anymore. That day was quite a turning point.

I made the conscious decision to follow my destiny and devote my life to this work. Yes, I was fortunate enough to be trained by some of the top mediums, and that training gave me the foundation of everything I've done since. For many people who aren't necessarily psychics or mediums, it's possible that they'll have their own calling cards from their loved ones.

◆⚜◆

One of the sayings I like to use is: "Those on the Other-Side want to talk to you as much as you want to talk to them!" There are so many ways in which they might try to get your attention, but for many people, the signs go unrecognized. Whether you're still feeling emotional due to a recent loss, or are just immersed in the business of life, it's easy to simply miss those little signs and symbols that they're trying to send you. The part of my work I love most is teaching my psychic-development workshops, to see people at the start of the weekend, completely unaware, and then watch them leave two days later with a more heightened consciousness. They've made new connections not only with themselves, but with their loved ones.

There are many different types of messages, signs, and symbols that those in Spirit use to tell us that they not only love us, but that they're still connected to us. These signs and symbols come in all shapes and sizes, and they can easily be missed in the wink of an eye.

Let's be clear what these signs and symbols are known as. They're called ADCs (after-death communications), which is a term I picked up from my colleagues Bill and Judy Guggenheim. They are the authors of the bestseller *Hello From Heaven!* While they were writing the book, they carried out extensive research and interviewed more than 3,300 people who believed they had been contacted by deceased relatives. More than 300 stories from their research are included in this fascinating book, and in my opinion, it completely validates everything that I do.

Of course, over the past 17 years, I've amassed a huge collection of my own beautiful stories and incidents from the hundreds of people who've had private readings with me, my students, and those who attend my lectures. I know that many have experienced first-hand communication from their loved ones. Bill and Judy's research reaches a powerful conclusion, in that an estimated 60 to 120 million Americans have had some form of an ADC experience.

These ADCs come in many forms, and it's important to stress here that they're *not* facilitated through a psychic or a medium or using a tool of any kind. These are spiritual experiences that just happen spontaneously and are usually quite personal. I believe when loved ones pass before we do, and once they settle again, they often do everything in their power to get our attention. When they do send a sign, what are they trying to tell us? Simply that they have survived death and that they love us and want us to continue to live our lives to the fullest.

During my lectures, I always try to devote some time to taking questions from the audience. It's a great way for people to ask those burning questions that have been on their minds but rarely get the chance to ask. I was in Seattle recently, and as I opened the floor to questions, a sea of hands shot up! A woman almost jumped out of her seat as she said, "John, I'm Elaine, and my question is this: Why don't my loved ones just show up in front of me?"

Even though it's a very serious topic, I've learned to mix in a little humor to lighten what can be a heavy subject, so my response that night got the usual warm reaction as I said, "Come on, Elaine, if your loved ones on the Other-Side suddenly popped up in front of you — what would happen?" I waited for the laughter to subside before carrying on. "First, your hair might turn white, and then you'd probably die from shock!"

I went on to explain how those on the Other-Side try to be quite subtle with their signs, mainly so you're not startled. "Now don't get me wrong," I continued. "Some people have seen a full apparition of their loved ones. I believe it's rare, but I know it happens, and like all ADCs, they are truly very special." I finished off answering the question by telling the audience about some of the many ways in which ADCs are sent, some of which I will tell you about here. I'll list some of the other ways later in this chapter.

### Dreams

Based on the information I gave that audience, it won't come as a surprise that the number one way that spirits come through is in your dreams. Why? Because when you're asleep, your mind isn't working overtime; it's calm and relaxed, and your analytical left-brain side takes a break. Those on the Other-Side can slip into your dreams, as this is the easiest way for them to softly step into your consciousness and psyche.

In almost all my lectures and workshops, I love to ask the audience: "Who's had a dream of their loved ones when you *know* for a fact that it really was them?" Half of the audience's hands will enthusiastically go up. Some people may have had this dream a week ago, a month ago; or even for some, many years may have passed since a loved one came to them in a dream. Here's the interesting part of this phenomenon: no matter how long ago the dream took place, the memory of that special ADC is often as fresh as though it were dreamed last night.

When I ask people to describe what happened in the dream, what was said, or how the person looked, the answers are usually always the same. First, they always appear healthy. If there was illness before they passed, if age ravaged their bodies, or even if they passed in an accident, no sign of this is evident in the dream. Often if they passed when they were elderly, they appear to look young and vibrant. They are smiling, happy, healthy, and perfect.

Many people have recounted their dreams, and they distinctly remember saying to their loved one, "What are you doing here — you're dead!" The messages that come back in the dream are usually short but often the same. Without opening their mouths, the spirits just use thoughts to convey that their soul lives on, and that they still love the person they're visiting. Most important, they actually *want* you to go on with your lives here, to be happy, and to know that they will see you again.

Of course, *not* every dream you have of loved ones is a true ADC. It may be that it's your own mind dealing with and working through your bereavement process, especially if the dream is disturbing or if the spirits are appearing in a negative way. You'll know which ones are true ADCs. They'll have a sense of clarity to them; they'll be more detailed, very loving, enjoyable; and above all, positive.

Those of you who've read my previous books know that I recommend that you keep a journal beside your bed to record your dreams. If you'd like to have an ADC dream about a loved one, then a good way to start is to spend some time in quiet reflection or meditation. Send the thought out to that person. Put all the love you have in your heart and think of him or her. Ask them to appear in your dreams, and tell them that you're ready and willing to receive a message. Remember, you may just get that person you're seeking, but don't be surprised if you actually get someone you least expect!

## Smells

Another common way in which spirits choose to come through is through *smells*. The sense of smell is one of our most powerful senses — whether it's the essence of fresh spring flowers, a particular perfume, freshly baked bread, or the whiff of a pungent cigar. Each smell imprints its unique impression on your memory bank. Scents have an amazing power to vividly bring back memories that you may have long forgotten. When we smell a freshly baked apple pie, it may bring up loving recollections of a grandmother, or the whiff of the ocean could conjure up happy days spent on your dad's boat. A man once told me that the smell of a freshly mowed lawn brought back childhood memories of family barbecues, as his dad always cut the grass before he started the grill!

Stop and ponder for a minute about what smells bring back special memories for you. If you put this book down for a moment and think about it, I'm sure you'll have your own memories of certain scents and how they spark a happy memory. Mine would have to be the aroma of my mom's Italian cooking and all the spices she used to tempt our palates. The smell of meatballs simmering in that delicious red sauce always brings back memories of my mom working in the kitchen, giving us samples as she cooked.

As I've already said, remember that when ADCs happen, they're very often quite subtle, particularly when related to scents. For example, if your dad used to smoke cigars in his lifetime, and one day for no reason you smell cigar smoke, don't be alarmed.

Obviously, check that there's no one in the house actually smoking a cigar. If not, then it might be your dad's way of saying, "Hi, I just wanted to let you know that I'm with you right now."

A woman told me how she often smells her mom's favorite cologne. Her first instinct was to yell at the kids, but she knew they'd deny touching that special bottle that belonged to her mom. I remember a friend of mine telling me a story about accompanying another medium to a local radio show for an interview. She was giving a message to one of the callers, telling her that the spirit who came through loved to smoke pipes. All of a sudden, the aroma of pipe tobacco filled the enclosed studio! I believe the host of the radio show was quite surprised, and I'm sure he'll never forget what happened that special evening. This is just another beautiful example of an ADC using smells to trigger a connection.

Know that someone is trying to get your attention if you have a similar experience. Too many of us try to rationalize them and explain them away. That's okay, too. When you're ready, it will happen, and then you'll recognize it for what it is. Just take your time.

Another story that I tell at all my lectures happened a few years ago when I was giving a program during one of our typical New England winters. I was totally surprised by how many people showed up since we had just had one of our heavy snowstorms, with more than ten inches falling in just a few hours.

Everyone had been in panic mode that morning as the snow piled up, but I was relaxed, as I knew that not even a storm could stop those on the Other-Side from making an appearance. The one thing about New England is that the roads are cleared really quickly. During the lecture, I was discussing how to recognize communication from the Other-Side. It was the part where I explained how to watch out for smells. I'd barely finished my sentence when a very young woman raised her hand and told me something that had just happened to her.

"John, I just want to share my story. My mom passed away a few years ago. She was always working in her garden," she explained. "It was a spectacular garden, which the neighbors and casual passersby all admired. In fact, she won a number of horticultural contests for her prize roses." She took a deep breath as her eyes began to well up with tears, and went on to tell the audience that a few days before this event, it was the anniversary of her mom's passing. She woke up that morning and realized that her entire house was filled with the sweet smell of her roses.

She went on, "John, trust me, I wasn't imagining it. I live alone now, so I'd know if I had bought some roses the day before, but I hadn't. Yet I'd been thinking a lot about my mom the night before, as it was the anniversary of her death." She went on to explain how initially, she'd struggled to make the connection and figure out where the smell of roses was coming from. When she'd finished telling this beautiful story, I asked her to come up onstage.

As I placed her face in my hands and looked straight into her tearful eyes, I asked her, "Darling, so what do you think that was?"

I thought the answer was almost a given, but what she said next surprised me and made the audience burst into laughter.

"I just thought it was the Glade air freshener coming in from one of my neighbors' homes!" she said.

Trying not to embarrass her, I replied, "You mean to tell me, that on the anniversary of your mom's passing — a woman known for her prize roses — your whole house fills with the scent of roses in the dead of winter and you honestly think that an air freshener could travel from one home to another, through two sets of double-glazed storm windows, and fill your house with that smell?" The audience giggled at the thought of this.

"Well, John, I didn't know what else to think," she said, as she lowered her head. I could see that she was embarrassed, so I gave her a huge hug.

"That was most likely your mom saying, 'I'm here with you today and I love you so very much,'" I said. The woman walked offstage with a smile that radiated through the entire auditorium, clearly thankful for her mom's message.

It's fascinating how often we try to explain everything away. Of course, not everything can be rationalized, especially when we're talking about the ways in which our loved ones still try to send us validations of their existence. If they were here physically, they'd be connecting to us; and sharing in our lives, loves, joys, sorrows, family birthdays and gatherings, holidays, anniversaries, and of course, our accomplishments. I genuinely believe that those on the Other-Side, given the chance, will never miss a good party! So remember, just because their souls are no longer in physical bodies, it doesn't mean they stop caring for or loving us.

### Finding Your Own Calling Cards

When someone passes and leaves this world, the normal and familiar way you communicate is interrupted for a time until a new form of communication is established, even though there can be a learning period for how it all works. There are so many different ways in which those on the Other-Side will try to get your attention. Besides dreams and smells, which are probably two of the most common that I hear about, there are other ways and means they'll use to send you signs, symbols, or messages. It could be as simple as a touch on the shoulder, a kiss on the cheek, a tousle of your hair, or even a tingle up your spine. When they really want to get your attention, they're going to do their utmost to get you to take notice so that you're aware of them and acknowledge that they're still connected to you.

Here are a few more examples of some of the most common types of ADCs:

### Feeling the Presence of Your Loved Ones

Many people who've lost a family member or friend, or even a beloved pet, may find themselves saying, "I may be going crazy, but I swear I feel them around me." We're so good at talking ourselves out of experiences that don't fit into stereotypical or more logical reasoning.

Next time you feel someone around you and you're questioning yourself, stop and try a different approach. Acknowledge their presence, say "Hello" or "I love you," and ask for another sign. They want to know if you can in fact feel them. It could be loving thoughts that they're sending; and by allowing your mind, body, and spirit to become receptors, you'll be able to pick up those special sentiments. Sadly, too many people think that their minds are just playing tricks on them or their imaginations are going into overdrive because they want a connection so desperately.

### Synchronistic Events

How often has this happened to you or someone you know? You're thinking of your mom, who passed some years ago, while you're driving home from work. Just at the exact moment her memory pops into your consciousness, you pull up behind another car, and there's a bumper sticker or license plate that says: "NBR 1 MOM." Or another scenario: at the exact moment you're thinking of your mom, you turn on the radio and there's her favorite song playing! Are you still trying to figure out how those on the Other-Side work this out with the disc jockey? To this day, I'm amazed at the lengths they'll go to to get your attention!

I remember once hearing from a gentleman who said that he was at the checkout counter at the supermarket, and as he was patiently waiting for his turn, a couple stepped in line behind him. He could clearly overhear them talking about their family. It was totally weird, as almost all the names they mentioned were in fact the same as the names of some of his own family members who had passed. He also told me that he could see that if they'd been common names like John or Mary, it wouldn't have registered with him, but some of his family names were quite unusual. In the end, he did turn around to take a quick glance and make sure that he wasn't related to this couple in some strange way.

Are these coincidences? I don't believe so. I often feel that those on the Other-Side can assist you in being in the right place at the right time, so when out of the blue you find yourself thinking of someone who has passed, maybe at that exact moment the person is lovingly thinking of *you*!

## Electricity

Lights flickering, television sets going on and off by themselves, radios and stereos acting up for no reason, electric clocks gaining or losing time or just stopping at the time of the person's death, cell phones registering the phone number of someone who's already passed — these are just a few examples of how spirits use electricity and energy to grab our attention. Whatever will they come up with next? I wouldn't be surprised if they begin to Twitter!

My friend Debra recently lost her dad after a very long illness, and then four months later she lost her mother. It's as if her mom followed her dad to the Other-Side. With two of the most important people in her life having passed, it was too much for Debra to take. One evening with tears in her eyes, she looked up and called out to her mother, "Mommy, if you can hear me, I really need a sign to let me know that you and Daddy are okay!"

Debra went to bed that night and was woken up by the alarm on her new BlackBerry phone. When she went to shut off the alarm, she didn't see the clock. All she noticed was the picture of her mother she'd taken months earlier! As she was telling the story, she swore that she hadn't programmed the picture to come up with the alarm. She explained that to access the images, you have to touch quite a few keys first. This was the sign she needed. She didn't ask for specifics, but asked her mother to send any sign she could. Her mom didn't let her down.

I heard from another woman whose dad always had to have the fan on. When other people got too cold, they'd shut it off, and of course, he'd turn it back on. After his passing, the fan would often turn on by itself, even when the house was empty!

I believe that since everything is made up of energy vibrating at its own unique frequency, including those on the Other-Side, electricity is a relatively easy way for them to use their energy to make things go on and off, and by doing so, make their presence known. As always, I want you to stay grounded with this. So, if your lightbulb is blinking — check the bulb or check your circuits. Not every flickering light is going to be an ADC. I want to make sure you've checked every physical reason before you jump to the conclusion that it's something paranormal.

### Pennies from Heaven

One of the more beautiful examples of an ADC is one of the most common ones. Yes, it's finding those odd pennies. I've asked audiences all over the world, "How many of you find pennies in odd places around the house, and in your heart you know they're from a loved one?" I'm usually met with a sea of waving hands. The stories I hear are often about the date on the penny being the same year of a loved one's passing or birth year. If you start finding pennies or dimes, notice the date. It could be significant. More often than not, no matter how old the coin is, people tell me that it's always shiny, as though it's fresh from the bank. Some people find pennies, while others find dimes, but rarely do people find quarters or, better still, silver dollars. Maybe some do find those, but pennies and dimes are the most common.

Now many people have said to me, "Come on, John, everyone finds coins!" Well, no. It's not how they communicate with me. Of course, people leave coins around or even toss them in the street, but I'm talking about finding pennies and dimes in places you've just visited — for instance, on the bed you just made, in the tub you just cleaned, on the dresser you just polished, on the floor you just vacuumed, or even on a path that you just walked along. Once you begin to find coins as you're thinking of someone in particular who has passed, you'd better get out a small piggy bank, because they'll keep coming when you need that validation from them. They will be your calling cards from heaven!

## Nature

Working with Mother Nature is one of the wonderful ways for those on the Other-Side to grab your attention. It could be birds, flowers, trees, butterflies, insects, water, rainbows, or some other animal. Many people connect with specific symbols when they think of a loved one. It could be something that you or a special person who has passed has a link to. Some feel that butterflies are their calling cards from a loved one. Butterflies are a great ADC because they are wonderful symbols of transformation and liberation — in the same way that their loved ones are free of their bodies.

We are all connected to each other as well as nature, so now you can understand why those on the Other-Side use the wonders of the earth as their calling cards. Let's have the usual reality check, in that not every bird you may see will be a loved one trying to get your attention. It could be just a bird! Mind you, if your dad loved blue jays, and one shows up on your windowsill at the precise moment you were thinking about your dad or missing him, then in fact that could be an ADC. My friend Gretchen knows that her calling card from her dad is a simple feather. Sometimes when she's really missing her dad, a feather will appear, no matter where she may be. She will look down and sure enough, there's a feather at her feet. She has often told me, though, that it's rarely more than one.

A few weeks ago, right at the end of a long winter, I was sitting in my home-based studio presenting my weekly radio show, when a woman called in to tell me a beautiful story about a neighbor whom she'd become close to, who'd suddenly passed away from an illness. Months earlier, the same neighbor had given her a rosebush for her garden as a gift. After she passed, and toward the end of the winter, this woman was lovingly thinking of her neighbor and missing the special "coffee talks" they often shared. For no reason, she felt drawn to peer into her backyard where she'd planted the rosebush, and to her utter amazement, there was one single rose that had bloomed through the snow!

This is the way loved ones, friends, and even neighbors give us signs of their gentle, loving guidance, which is always around us. When we're open, it's much easier to receive a message that's meant specifically for us.

## Numbers

Numbers play a key role in our lives, in the world, in science, and in technology. When you think of it, everything in the universe revolves around numbers — from the rotation of the earth and the planets, to our calendars, to the way we keep time.

Do numbers keep showing up in *your* life? Some people who have ADCs through numbers will see the same figures repeatedly, whether it's on a digital clock, a license plate, dollar bills, telephone numbers, or those synchronistic moments when you find you have the same birthday as someone you've just met. Many people will see the exact time of the passing of a loved one repeatedly appearing in their lives.

Numbers play a big part in my work, both on- and offstage. For a while, I frequently used to see the number 149. No matter what order they were in, these three numbers kept popping up in my life. I searched my memory bank and scrambled the numbers in every possible combination. For the life of me, I couldn't figure out what it meant. No one I knew had passed at that specific time, nor did any birth dates make sense. So, I figured they were given to me to play the lottery. Well, sadly, that didn't work either.

Then, I noticed that every time I was on my way to demonstrate, I'd always see those same numbers. Sometimes I'd notice them on a license plate, a billboard, or on the side of a bus. There they were again! It finally dawned on me that they were "my guides" checking in with me, letting me know that they were going to be with me. It was comforting to know they were there. In those early days, I suffered from stage fright before an event, wondering if the link would still be there. I've been doing this work for more than 17 years now, and thankfully, it just grows stronger. Nowadays, when I see these numbers, I simply say "Hello" and thank my guides for the confirmation.

Some numbers, like 149, may mean nothing to you. However, I would recommend a great book by Doreen Virtue called *Angel Numbers,* which explains some of the meanings behind different number sequences. Keep a note in your journal when you notice your special numbers, and try to remember what you were just *thinking* or what you were just *doing.* The numbers might be nothing more than confirmation that you're on the right track. Then again, they could have greater significance.

Numbers that continue to show up may not always be from someone who has passed, for they could just be from your guides, your angels, your intuition, or the universe. Once you begin to notice and understand numbers, you'll never look at them in the same way again.

## Missing Items

I truly believe that those on the Other-Side love to play with us when they're trying to grab our attention. How many times have you just put down your ring, necklace, watch, wallet, keys, or even your eyeglasses, only to find that when you went back to get them, they're gone! You find yourself saying: "I *know* I just left them here." You begin to search high and low, driving yourself crazy. Then, of course, you know what happens. The same place you just looked only moments before, the same place you thought you'd left them, is where they were all along . . . or were they? You think, *I must have missed them when I was looking before.*

This happens too often to too many people for it to be a coincidence. This is yet another example of an ADC. Just as those on the

Other-Side can leave us gifts, they also can make things disappear and reappear. Why do they do so? It's just their way of saying, "Hi, I am here." Quite often, it's someone who had a sense of humor while he or she was alive, and apparently, we don't lose that part of ourselves over there.

So the next time this happens to you, yes, you could be just forgetful — as always, stay grounded with this — but think for a moment, and ask yourself, *Who do I know who has passed that could be playing with me?* This could be their comical calling card meant just for you.

◆✻◆

These are just a few examples of the hundreds of different ways in which your loved ones may try to get your attention, and trust me — they will try anything to reach out to you. No matter what ADCs you may receive, they're always meant to be loving, joyful, and positive experiences — ones that give you hope and comfort, and are usually received exactly when you need them. They shouldn't be scary or frightening, or cause you more grief. Just to repeat once again, it's their way of saying "I love you, and I am with you always."

If you believe in ADCs but have yet to experience one, I've learned that those in Spirit often take their cues from you. If they know that you're still emotional and that an ADC may upset you, they might pass a message through someone else until you're ready to receive one directly yourself.

When you feel you're really open and ready to receive, put a loving thought out to the spirit world and ask them to show you a sign, one that you'll know is from them. Please keep an open mind so that you don't have set expectations of what you want it to be. It may be the same sign over and over, or it could be different every time. Trust me, they know when you're ready and how to get your attention. Be thankful for them, cherish them, and hold them close to your heart, for they truly are *calling cards from heaven.*

# CHAPTER 10

# SENSITIVE CHILD —
# PSYCHIC CHILD

The innocence, honesty, and sensitivity of children are truly precious gifts. In this new millennium and the latter part of the last century, there's a whole new generation of children. Some say that they're here to help the world, whereas others think that the human genetic code is changing. I don't have any set opinion, but for all I know, this could be the reason why the awareness of these kids is expanded far beyond what we have ever known in the history of humankind. Are these children living proof of our unlimited human potential? From what I am witnessing and hearing now, I believe they are.

The Psychic Generation is here. I've become fascinated by the ever-increasing numbers of children who are displaying amazing psychic abilities, and I've noticed over the past few years how many questions I get at my lectures, on my radio show, and through e-mail about psychically sensitive children. The other day, I was giving one of my special "Gatherings" lectures, where I get to talk and demonstrate my mediumship to a smaller group in a more intimate, connected environment. It's truly a bonding experience, as everyone in the room shares in each other's pain and sorrow, and also laughs together. This particular evening, a hand flew up in the back of the room when I asked if anyone had a question about psychic development, the afterlife, or spirituality. A woman frantically waved both her arms in the air, and then jumped to her feet and yelled out, "John! Please help me! My child is very psychically sensitive, and I don't know how I can help her."

More and more people are seeking information to help their children who seem a little different. There are so many more books about psychic children now, and there's a lot more support than I had when I was a boy. However, some parents know that their children may need help and support beyond their capabilities, and I'm *not* talking about medication. I've received hundreds of e-mails and letters asking for advice on how to tell if a child is highly sensitive or psychically gifted. Some parents even ask me to help them nurture those children who show signs of psychic ability or who have highly sensitive natures. Children are our most precious gifts, not just for us, but for the planet. They are our future. What they experience here and now in the present will profoundly affect them in the years to come.

In those wonderful early formative years, where innocence abounds, I believe that young children see the world as it *truly* is. Children have a way of showing their sensitivity in such simple ways. For example, if your child encounters someone new and it appears that he doesn't like that person, then I'd always suggest that first and foremost, you take a moment to listen closely. He may even say, "Mommy, I don't like their colors." What might be happening here is that your child may be able to *see* clairvoyantly, or he's *feeling* the colors emanating from that person's aura.

When you ask your child why he's saying this, he may not be able to explain himself or why he's feeling what he's feeling. He could just be picking up the energy of the person, and he interprets it as something that he's not comfortable with. The important thing is that you're totally supportive and don't condemn the behavior as being rude. Remain open-minded, and talk to your child about what he's feeling and experiencing.

Children are even more sensitive than adults. Someone wrote to me with a story about a parent who was constantly pointing a finger at her daughter when she was upset with the girl. On one occasion, a relative who had clairvoyant skills was in the room when this happened, and she could see what was really happening. Clearly, the upset mother was pointing her finger at the child, but in reality, she was actually stabbing the child's aura. The little girl, being very sensitive, reacted accordingly and displayed increased signs of irritation and discomfort. It just goes to show you how sensitive children are, and at one time as kids ourselves . . . so were we.

### Experiences of the Psychic Child

Thousands of children who are psychically aware suffer in silence as a result of being highly sensitive. Many don't know whether they're normal or not. All too often, they're made to feel different; and in the most severe cases, they can even suffer from feeling unloved and end up retreating into an introverted state for self-preservation. If left unnoticed, they can feel left out, resulting in low self-esteem and other long-term problems. I've heard of children being teased continually, which can lead to withdrawal and isolation. I speak with some experience when I say that without the proper training — usually by parents or teachers — these children will find it uncomfortable and even difficult to survive in such a chaotic, boisterous world.

The best way to offer insight is to explain what it's like to feel different. I'm not ashamed to tell my story, and I hope that in the years I've spent baring my soul onstage and in my books, in some small way I've helped people understand what it's like to grow up being sensitive. If I've done that, then it's all been worth it.

I'm the second of five children, born into an Italian-Irish Catholic family in the 1960s in Boston. The only reason why I mention being the second child is that I have many friends who are the second born, and many are equally sensitive. Out of all of us, even as a young boy, I was the one curled up in the window with my nose stuck in some book about religion, magic, esoteric studies, or spirits and ghosts. My brothers and the other neighborhood kids would be outside playing sports and generally getting into mischief. Yet I was quite happy being alone in my own inner world. It was a sort of sanctuary, a place where

I could use my imagination and spiritual gifts. I used this special place to retreat to when I needed to feel safe.

Most children who are psychically sensitive will often retreat to their inner world. For example, if you see a child just staring at the plants and flowers in a garden as though they're in a daydream, then I believe they're connecting to nature in a different way from most of the world. What may appear as simply a flower to many — will be totally different to the psychic child. These kids could be watching the energy and colors that swirl around all living things. It's as though they have their own personal connection with the natural world that's all around them.

It's said that some children can even observe the world of the "elementals," which are basically Nature Spirits (also known as fairies) that can be called upon or summoned. In the purely environmental sense, they are nonhuman beings; and are often linked to the four elements of air, water, fire, and earth. If they choose to show themselves to you, they may select a form that you will recognize and be comfortable with, or they may pick something that's associated with the element they represent. Typically, a fire elemental may appear as a spark or a flickering face in a flame. Equally, the water elemental may be a cold spot when you're swimming in the ocean. An air elemental could be a sudden breeze or tiny whirlwind in the dust. That piece of stone in your shoe could be a sign of the earth elementals at play.

Just because most people are not seeing, hearing, or feeling what your child is experiencing, who are we to say that it doesn't exist? Even as a young boy, I was fascinated by anything and everything related to this magical world. While I read avidly, I was also drawing and experimenting with color. I'd sometimes pick up my sketchbook and before I knew it, I would have drawn some scene as though I'd been there the day before. I never really knew where the inspiration came from, but the sense of familiarity of a scene, the palette of colors, or some shape would somehow resonate with me. I'd never had any formal training, and to this day, I wonder where my gift of drawing came from. My mother still jokes with me about how my father used to look at me, shake his head, and say to her, "Something's wrong with *your* son!" Since when did I just become her kid?

### Do You Have a Psychically Sensitive Child?

To have a psychically sensitive child, you must be *willing* to have a psychically sensitive child. How can these abilities or talents be understood, developed, and used? Rather than looking to the child for answers, we must first be aware of the attitudes, thoughts, and feelings of their parents and teachers, who must realize that being intuitive or psychic is normal. There are too many misconceptions about the word *psychic,* so let me try to apply some clarity and meaning to it all. The word *psychic* comes from the Greek word *psychos,* meaning "of the soul." What this actually means is that as spiritual beings, we are able to access, receive, and transmit information that reaches beyond our physical bodies and our natural five senses. As I've said earlier, as children we're completely free to experience things, without the constraints that come later in life. It's usually when we start school that external influences start to have their effects.

Most children are quite intuitive or psychic until the age of seven. If you want to see souls in action, then watch children as they enjoy their early years without a care in the world. In those first few years, they haven't fully integrated into the physical world; it's as if they have one foot here and one foot still in the Spirit world. In reality, they're living their lives through the creative, intuitive right-hand side of the brain — a place of imagination, magic, and wonder.

School soon begins for children; and with it a more structured, logical, and traditional approach to thinking. Children start to adapt and focus more on their parents, teachers, books, and learning as they begin to cope with the external influences of society. This is when the more analytical left side of the brain becomes the predominant force and is used more. For many children, it's a completely natural transition as they slowly begin to pull away from their right-brain creative side; and as a result, they become less aware of their intuition and psychic ability or simply forget about it, as they integrate into the physical world.

Some children, like myself, never lose that special connection with their sensitivity and have to learn to live with their gifts, talents, and abilities just like everybody else.

Do you wonder if you have a psychically sensitive child? I hope that the description of my own experience and some of the information in this chapter will help you understand the needs of these sensitive souls.

Here are just a few of the typical signs of a sensitive psychic child. Do any of these fit your child? If they do, then you could well have a son or daughter who needs your care and special attention.

- Startles easily
- Does not react well to surprises
- Seems to know what others are thinking
- Feels overwhelmed or agitated in noisy environments
- Is highly sympathetic to others — especially other children
- Feels more deeply about things than most kids
- Seems to sense what others are feeling
- Prefers quiet play or being on his or her own
- Doesn't do well with sudden changes
- Seems to have an active inner life
- Often asks deep, thought-provoking questions
- Dreams of flying
- Often talks about being out of his or her body and viewing things from above
- Experiences highly vivid dreams that quite often come true
- Has the ability to communicate with animals and nature
- Communicates with angels
- Sees faces while trying to go to sleep
- Is highly artistic or creative

### *Imaginary Friends*

Many children often mention having an *imaginary friend* whom they talk to or play with. A close friend of mine is still teased by his family, as his mom used to set a place at the dinner table for his "imaginary" friend, and he wouldn't start to eat until his friend sat next to him! Are they imaginary or are they the spirits of other children or even relatives who have passed? Most parents will probably try to nip this in the bud, but if you have a child who seems to have an imaginary friend, instead of telling her to stop making up stories, try asking, "Does this person have a name?" "What does the person look like?" "What is he wearing?" or "What is he saying to you?" You might be surprised when your child comes up with a name or even describes a relative, such as a grandparent, whom she's never seen before.

My client Margaret told me about her daughter, Emma. She was pretty calm about the whole situation, and told me that Emma would wake up at odd times of the night. It was always for the same reason: to tell her mom that the "old lady" was in her room again. When Margaret got up and looked around her daughter's room, as always, no one was there. Margaret didn't know what else to say and would just tell her daughter to go back to sleep and that she must be dreaming.

The weeks turned into months, and Emma continued to tell her mom the same thing, until one day she blurted out, "Mommy, the old lady's name is Grace." The name was quite a surprise to Margaret, for the only Grace she'd ever known in her life was an elderly neighbor who used to baby-sit her when she was a little girl, while her parents both worked late. Curiosity got the better of her, and Margaret rummaged around in the attic to find a box of old photos. Eventually, she found what she was looking for, and sat staring at an old photo of Grace with Margaret as a child, holding some cotton candy at a local carnival.

She deliberated for a while, and then tentatively showed the picture to Emma. Her little face lit up with instant recognition, as she jumped up and down excitedly screaming, "That's my Gracie, Mommy! That's my Gracie!" Well, I think it's obvious that Grace is looking out for Emma now, just as she did for Margaret.

When I was a child, there would be nights when I'd lie awake in bed and see "spirit people," shadowy figures with kind faces that often had a sort of illumination around them. They'd just be walking through my bedroom, appearing and disappearing. From my first encounter with them, they didn't scare me at all. In a funny sort of way, I actually looked forward to seeing them. Strangely, they went out of their way to look at me warmly, and sometimes they'd simply nod a little hello just to let me know they'd seen me there. I didn't know who these people were, but I felt comforted and protected by their presence.

### Tips for Parents

I want to reiterate that, as we're all psychic, children need our guidance to show them that being intuitive or sensitive is quite natural. Imagine you're having a heated discussion or an argument with someone, and your child just walks into the house. You see him at the door and stop talking. The child asks if everything is all right. You go on to say, "Yes, honey, everything is fine. Now go and do your homework."

So what's wrong with this scenario? What you've actually done is encourage your child *not* to trust his intuition. The child was picking up the energy from your argument and probably didn't understand the unpleasant feelings he was sensing. The better scenario would be to tell the child that you're working out a problem and to let him know it will be fine. Then the child can acknowledge his intuition and discard the feelings in the knowledge that's there's no major issue. There are so many things that parents can do to assist their sensitive or psychic child. A good place to start is to *believe them!*

When I was a kid, it was hard for parents and teachers to understand exactly why was I so sensitive; and they struggled to explain how I saw, heard, and felt the things that most children did not. Luckily for children today, there are so many more books and television shows, as well as intuitive psychic adults and even organizations that are beginning to work with sensitive and psychic children. This is truly fantastic, and the most important part is that it will demonstrate that they're just like everyone else — just gifted in another way.

Here are some additional ways to help your child:

— **Be an aware and observant parent.** One useful way to do so is to start keeping a journal of what your child is saying, dreaming, or experiencing, especially if it's beyond what you consider normal. For example, record predictions made by your child; or if he's seeing angels, spirits, or so-called imaginary friends. I also recommend if your child is old enough, to encourage him to start writing in his own journal. A journal is a wonderful place where he can feel safe writing, drawing, and expressing what he's experiencing. Of course, I suggest that you ask permission before looking at that journal. If you're able to do so, you might begin to see how his intuitive mind works. Remember, we're all different, and so are the many ways in which your child will pick up and interpret his own psychic language.

— **Be a good listener.** When your child comes to you and says she's *feeling* a certain way about something or someone, don't push her away or trivialize the comment, but try to ask a few probing questions. I often tell parents that if a child is seeing someone in her room, then ask: "What does the person look like? Is it a male or female? What did he say to you? What is he wearing? Were you frightened? Did you see anything else?" If it's *not* a positive experience, it's important to ask why. "Did this frighten you? Do you feel scared when you see these things? Why are you saying that?" Let her know that she's always in control of these experiences. Over time, you can learn how to help your child turn down her sensitivity.

As a side note, I find it helpful for parents to learn all they can about the energy centers (chakras) of the body. Every chakra affects a different part of the body and specific psychic centers.

These energy centers all have different colors that can be opened and closed, and teaching children to "turn down their lights" will in turn help them turn down their psychic sensitivity.

— **Do not be a psychic stage mother or father.** In other words, don't turn it into a show! When I was a child, I was born with a rare gift for drawing, and my father used to make me draw on command. Part of me hated being put on show like this, and although he encouraged my creativity, forcing me to draw eventually took the fun and spontaneity out of it. I've heard stories of parents who've even made their children do spot readings for their friends, even when the children weren't ready. It can actually be dangerous to force a child to perform like this with no guidance or training. You might be proud of your psychic child, but trust me when I say that it's important for him to learn at an early age to respect his ability, and there's a time and a place for everything.

— **Provide a safe place to be.** From time to time, all sensitive and psychic children need a place where it's quiet and peaceful, preferably in a room with soft pastel colors. Colors affect us all, and some, such as vivid yellows or bright reds, can actually stimulate their sensitivity and cause them to feel agitated. I've discovered that children who have a fish tank in their rooms can often feel more relaxed, because when they gaze at the tank, it has a calming, meditative effect. Walking through the woods or a meadow, or even a quiet day on the beach, can yield equally wonderful benefits. Try to notice if your child is more relaxed or hyper in the different rooms of your home. You might just have to make different arrangements for where your children spend most of their time.

— **Teach them to take good care of their bodies.** Explain to your children why it's so important to eat well, exercise, and take time to play as well as making time to relax. When you're highly sensitive, intuitive, or psychic, then your body is like one big, highly tuned psychic antenna. Parents and teachers *have* to learn that human anatomy is a complex network of etheric wiring.

It's through this network that energy flows, and it's important to keep the body healthy if you wish to keep everything flowing. When I demonstrate, I often tell the audience before I start, "I'm the equipment — everything goes *through* me." So it's important to teach children how to ground themselves and to educate them about chakras so they're able to let the energy come in and flow out again. Above all, this will keep them balanced and firmly in the physical world.

— **Read upon, or take a class yourself on, psychic development.** Learn as much as you can (while staying grounded) about how psychic ability works. Learn to understand what psychic strengths children may have. They could be clairvoyant (to see), or clairsentient (to feel), or even clairaudient (to hear). There are different abilities, and each one has its own unique way of functioning. Another great way of sharing and learning is to belong to a community. There are many online communities for parents as well as psychic children. Reach out to people who understand what you're going through, and who you feel might be experiencing a similar set of circumstances. By talking and sharing, you'll help each other.

### A Place of Light

These children are here right now, and many more are on the way. I firmly believe that intuitive and psychically sensitive children are being born in ever-increasing numbers. It's vitally important that they're welcomed, understood, and taught to appreciate that their psychic gifts are not only there to help them, but just as important, to help those around them.

During my travels as a spirit whisperer, I discovered an extraordinary place especially for children, which is appropriately named A Place of Light. It's a beautiful haven in Cherry Valley, Massachusetts, where psychic and sensitive children can be in a safe, educational, and loving environment. Moreover, it's a place for them to express themselves as they explore and develop their gifts. They're *not* made to feel different — just educated in the knowledge that we're all born with different talents and abilities. How I wish I'd been able to go to a special place like this as a child!

A Place of Light allows the children who attend (often with their parents) to work with and honor their true selves. The center is not only dedicated to supporting intuitive children and their families, but it also helps intuitive adults. It's a place where parents and children can speak freely to experienced advisors, and particularly where the parents can discuss their children's experiences.

As a society, we seem to find ever-increasing ways of labeling some new behavioral disorder, so A Place of Light offers a wonderful forum to discuss your personal frustrations with labels such as ADHD, ADD, autism, and other such emotive terms. I believe that many behaviors that are labeled as being mental illnesses are actually manifestations of intuitive abilities.

There could be a center like this near you, and it's well worth doing some research if you have a highly sensitive child who might be afraid to go to sleep at night or refuses to go near certain parts of your home. These types of experiences are more than likely connected to a psychic experience.

I spoke with cofounders Susan Gale and Steve Lucero, who prefer not to put labels on these children. Susan told me that many people might have heard intuitive psychic children labeled as Indigo Children, Star Children, Crystal Children, or even Rainbow Children. She also explained that as far as they were concerned, these are just children who are tuned in beyond the normal five senses. In other words, they are psychically awake.

A television producer once asked me if I knew any psychic children, as she was thinking about producing a series featuring these special children and their gifts. Of course, I suggested that she take a look at A Place of Light. The show *Psychic Children: Their Sixth Sense* continues to air to this day. I'm glad to say that it's done an excellent job of showing how these kids are special and unique, and have all types of different abilities. Most important, it dispels some of the common misperceptions about these kids.

### Founding A Place of Light

Susan Gale was largely responsible for founding and establishing A Place of Light, and as a result, she comes with an impressive record of accomplishment. A former student of Edgar Cayce, she has devoted her entire professional life to working with children as a teacher, camp counselor, and administrator. When we met, she told me a lot about her past and her beliefs, many of which I share, such as how some people come into your lives for specific reasons and act as spiritual change agents. These could be fleeting visits, or a person could be part of your life for many years. There's no set timetable, and often this spiritual change agent can have a profound influence on your life, which ultimately moves you in a whole new direction. Susan told me about her spiritual change agent, and in her case, he was only three years old!

"I met this little boy who'd been labeled autistic. When I saw him for the first time, his eyes seemed to be saying something quite different, that he was very much connected to the present," she explained. She went on to tell me how she called upon her resident expert, her son, David, who is a gifted telepath, for help. David agreed to speak to the child, and the story she then told me left me deeply moved.

"You know, John, to watch what happened was truly amazing," Susan continued. "The boy began talking telepathically to my son, David, about how silly he thought people were to use such a slow way of communicating. He was referring to speaking aloud, of course!"

Susan went on to tell me how the little boy had explained to David that in a past life, he'd been an engineer in the army charged with the responsibility of designing catapults. She smiled as she told me that it probably had a lot to do with his passion for flinging things over walls! David had spent a lot of time with him, patiently explaining about today's world and encouraging the little boy to start trying to speak in spite of any clumsiness.

It was probably this experience that made Susan wonder how many other children were getting lost in the system. She clarified what she meant by telling me that she thought the system probably didn't recognize gifts beyond the basic five senses. Having established a school before, she wondered if a center could be created that addressed the needs of psychically gifted children. She wrote to Atlantic University in Virginia Beach, which introduced her to her current colleague and partner, Peggy Day.

Clearly this was the sign Susan needed, as Peggy had traveled the world and had been involved in helping many people find their spiritual paths, and she was also well grounded in the Edgar Cayce readings. Recently, Peggy received her master's degree in transpersonal studies from Atlantic University, and believes to this day that establishing A Place of Light was part of her life's purpose.

Wishing to receive direction only from the highest sources, Susan and Peggy have diligently persisted in seeking Divine guidance. Together, they continue to look for ways to help Spirit provide a place where children can freely discuss their spiritual gifts in a safe environment, and discover how they can develop and use their gifts for positive outcomes.

Their courses combine meditation with more practical skills, such as drama and gardening. They also teach children how to work with their dreams. They educate them on minerals and crystals, sending and receiving psychic impressions, American Indian traditions, how to understand the meanings and uses of colors, and most important, how to take care of their bodies.

These programs not only help the children, but also educate their parents and teachers in a community of like-minded individuals. I love the saying that describes their community: "There is strength in numbers. When a child can meet another sensitive child or a parent can talk to another parent who's confused about how to help their sensitive or psychic child, they can see they are never truly alone."

I will continue to do all I can for A Place of Light, for I feel their mission is so close to my heart. They encourage children to realize that they're not special or different; they're just gifted in their own way. The world does not have to be confusing or overwhelming for these children. When kids begin to understand their own psychic makeup and see that they're not alone, the world can be a wondrous place.

Finally, please remember that no matter how special or how amazing their abilities, these children are first and foremost *children*. Don't wrap them too tightly in a safety blanket. Try not to *over*protect them; after all, they have to learn to live in the physical world. Don't put them on a pedestal, but teach them to play, to have fun, and to enjoy their youth. Treat them like any other children, listen to them, and create a nurturing and safe environment for them. Let them know they can confide in you at any time and share what they're experiencing or feeling. When you do this, you'll forge a stronger bond that will go way beyond just being a parent — you'll become a friend.

These children are our future. Hopefully, the rest of humanity will understand this and allow these kids to make our world a safer, greener, healthier, and more peaceful place for us all!

# CHAPTER 11

# REINCARNATION —
# THE SOUL ETERNAL

As everything in this world is perpetually moving, change is
inevitable. It's the same for your soul, as you're constantly
evolving and moving forward with grace and humility on your
way to somewhere, whether you realize it or not. Throughout each
lifetime, you will experience and absorb *all* memories, feelings,
emotions, as well as your own unique personality, into your soul.
As I've said in my previous books, it's only the physical body, which
is just an overcoat, that actually dies. Once it's no longer needed,
it's discarded. However, the soul (the *real* you) truly does goes on.
It's only upon reaching the Spirit World that your soul can rest —
sometimes for a short period of time — while in other instances,
it could be longer before it can be reborn again and return to this
physical world. Life is and always will be continuous.

Every decision and choice you've made in past lives, and
especially those you're making in this present life, will influence
your soul's journey in the future. Your soul knows what it needs to
evolve and will often steer or even push you in the direction that it
wants for its highest good. Of course, there will be occasions when
you don't always follow its prompts, but trust me when I say that
it *will* continue to nudge you and guide you as you move forward
in this life.

It would be hard not to ignore the fact that humankind's
interest in all things spiritual is constantly growing, changing,
and evolving. One of the most commonly asked questions in my

lectures is "What happens to the soul?" which is quickly followed by the second part of the question, namely, "How often are people aware of previous lifetimes in their current souls' imprints?"

A good friend once told me that he felt he'd been a scribe in a French monastery hundreds of years ago, and now he's a professional writer! More and more people are beginning to question their souls' mortality and share a belief that they've lived in other lifetimes.

I believe in reincarnation for all sorts of reasons. How often have you experienced that incredible moment when you meet someone whom you feel you've either met before, or whose familiarity gives you the feeling that you've known each other your entire life? How do you explain that? Why do they seem so familiar? Why do you feel so much more at ease with some people on initial meetings than others? No matter how much you try to remember where you met them, the memory just eludes you.

Of course, it's not just about people; it's as much about places. Objects all leave their memory imprint on the soul. For example, you can be in a different country for the first time yet feel you've been there before, as though you've walked the streets and breathed in the air. Even gazing at a picture or a painting could evoke strong emotions. There's an innate sense of knowing.

It was some 15 years ago when I first experienced this phenomenon. It was the time an opportunity came up to leave the United States and spend some time in the UK. I was racked with indecision, and I remember how nervous I felt about leaving my home country and going to England to study and develop my mediumship. Should I or shouldn't I? I'd never traveled much, let alone to Europe, and really knew little about it, apart from watching a few television shows from the UK. I didn't even know many people from England, yet as soon as I arrived, I felt really comfortable, almost *too* comfortable. It was an amazing feeling, something that came from deep within me. I'm not talking about a conscious feeling that I could articulate, but more of a feeling that I'd been there before, yet it was so hard to express in simple words or thoughts.

The last few days in L.A. preparing to leave were manic. Then there was an 11-hour flight, followed by a 3-hour car ride from Heathrow Airport just outside London. I finally arrived in Bristol, totally jet-lagged, and promptly got a very bad cold. What a way to arrive! Looking back now, I remember being there barely two or three days when I found myself asking why it was that I felt so comfortable from the minute I'd landed in Britain. Why was I so at peace? Why did everything feel so familiar, the stone buildings rich in warm sandstone textures and their gray-slate or red-tiled roofs? Even the dampness of the air with the unfamiliar drizzle that's so synonymous with England felt comforting, as strange as that sounds! Maybe it was the rolling, emerald green hills that stretched on for miles, or just the sense of ease I felt as I started to connect with the people and their culture. It was as though every-thing about England had been etched in my mind and soul.

Fortunately, my cold didn't last long, and within days I was off exploring and quickly started to forge new friendships. One of my favorite haunts was this little coffee shop at the top of a steep hill, where I would idle away an hour or so, immersed in a book, curled up on one of their distressed sofas or an old armchair. It was heaven for me. People noticed that I was obviously American from the telltale baseball cap or my accent, but in the same breath would comment on how I seemed to just get along with everyone.

Considering that I'd had an extremely different upbringing, I was surprised by how well I took to their customs. I quickly became accustomed to the British way of life, as if I'd lived there my entire life. I wasn't remotely fazed by their quirky dry sense of humor or their strange mannerisms, and of course I'd be remiss if I didn't acknowledge the great British reserve. I quickly became "Anglophiled," as I sampled the meat pies and of course, the fish and chips! I even enjoyed the weather, even though I'd complain whenever it was cold, being dramatic with my statements, such as: "It's bone-chillingly cold!" It didn't take long for me to realize that in some past lifetime, I must have lived in England, even if it had been hundreds of years earlier.

### Soul Groups — Don't I Know You?

Even from an early age, I've always found the subject of reincarnation intriguing. I read books on the topic and found myself constantly asking questions about it. The belief in reincarnation is an ancient phenomenon and literally means "to be made flesh again."

Many people as well as religious sects believe in the continuity of the soul. It's a widely held belief that we actually reincarnate over and over to help the progression, evolution, and advancement of our souls. It's also said that we reincarnate in *soul groups*, which means that the people around us, such as family members, friends, and maybe even some of the people we work with, could have been with us in another lifetime.

Taking that logic one step further, your child at one time may have been your parent, even though that might be harder to fathom. You must have known a wise child at some time or another who seemed like such an advanced soul in such a young body. I've witnessed children who often seem to lead their parents; it's almost like a total role reversal where they take on the opposite role. Stop for a moment and ask yourself if you have a friend who feels more like a sibling. You experience different relationships within your soul group, and I believe that if you switch roles within your relationships, then on a purely soul level, it allows you to have a better understanding of the dynamics of what it was like to play out a certain role in a specific lifetime.

We all have a soul group that we're spiritually connected to. It's my belief that we're with that same group in the Spirit World. It's totally our choice whether we choose to meet up again to work or play together here in this physical world. The members of our soul group may well come into our lives at different times. Some may come in quickly and leave, while others will stay with us for our entire lifetimes. Again, I feel we prearrange this in the Spirit World and agree in advance how and when we're going to meet again, and what role or relationship will be played out this time.

As always, it's important that you forge your own views on this highly complex and emotive subject, and not just take my word or personal beliefs as gospel. If nothing more, it will certainly provide for lively debates at the dinner table!

So, how do you recognize your soul group members? I wish it were as simple as saying they're going to wear badges saying, "I'm part of your soul group." But I'm sure that when you meet one of them, you'll have a sense of knowing, a feeling that somehow you're connected on a deeper spiritual level. You'll discover that you have the same beliefs and ideas, and you're simply drawn to them spiritually.

It would be easy to get carried away here, painting a picture of perfection, but it's important to remember that there also might be times when you find yourself in a difficult relationship. For all you know, it could be one that you and a certain member prearranged to play out in this lifetime. Perhaps it's to fix some unresolved issue or dispute from the past, or just to heal an old wound.

These difficult relationships are just as important as the positive ones. We learn so much from them, as often they're the catalysts that enable us to grow, or sometimes they help us move in a new direction. With each lifetime, the soul continues to learn, transform, grow, and evolve as we become more spiritually attuned and grow ever closer to the Divine Source.

You are the total accumulation of *all* your soul's experiences through different lifetimes; and all these situations, relationships, and human interactions create the history of your soul and leave their imprint. Some of the lessons that you may need to learn in this lifetime may never be dealt with. Equally, there will be lessons that you attempt to learn but may need to be addressed in another lifetime for whatever the reason. A lesson unlearned has the tendency to be repeated even louder the next time, until you do in fact get it! The education and progression of the soul doesn't end when you die; it continues to evolve. When you leave this world, you continue to learn and grow but just on a higher spiritual plane.

I try to remain open-minded, rather than live a life being skeptical or closed-minded. However, the big question is this: Is reincarnation real, and if it's true, do we have to keep coming back? I've read and studied this subject for many years, but there's nothing like firsthand experience to put it all into perspective. I had a wonderful opportunity to experience my *own* past-life regression. Here's my story.

### *My Journey Back*

Some people make a conscious decision to be regressed back to a past life in the hopes of seeing why they're experiencing difficulties in this lifetime, or to better understand personal-relationship issues.

Experiencing a past life can certainly be enlightening. If you or someone you know is having difficulty here and you believe a past-life regression would be therapeutic, then as long as the person is open, I'd certainly give it a try. As always with any type of therapy, make sure you work with a trained and bona fide therapist. Do your research and check references if you're not sure. If your interest is one of pure curiosity or because you think it might be fun, then remember that it's *this* life where you should focus your concern. This life at this time, at this very moment, is what's important. What you do today will affect what you do or don't do in another life.

Many of you may have heard of my colleague and friend Brian Weiss, M.D. He's a psychiatrist who lives in Miami, Florida. His reputation precedes him, and his credentials are impressive, having graduated from Columbia University and Yale Medical School, as well as being former chairman of psychiatry at Mount Sinai Medical Center in Miami. He's also the author of the bestseller *Many Lives, Many Masters.*

I'm always delighted when we work together, as I feel privileged to take the stage with the man who brought reincarnation and past-life-regression therapy into the 20th and 21st centuries. While we've lectured together many times, when possible I still try to listen to his fascinating presentation and take part in his group regressions.

He begins by setting the mood with his soft, calming voice, and then slowly begins to relax everyone before he begins the regression. He takes everyone back to the womb, where this life started, before we are physically born. No matter how many times I tried to go beyond this point, I'd fall asleep, or I'd let my mind wander off into some sort of trance. All too often at the end of the lecture, I'd hear the most wonderful stories of what others had experienced, but all I could remember in the meditation was barely getting to my mother's womb, and then blank!

Lately, I've been asking myself questions about my work and the reason why I was drawn to it, but more important, where it's taking me. I tried seeking spiritual guidance from my guides, and even sought clarity about certain relationships in my life. I knew there was another opportunity coming up to work with Brian at the Omega Institute in Rhinebeck, New York. When we were chatting on the phone one night, I told him how I always trance out and never remember anything about my experiences in his group regressions. He offered to do a one-on-one full regression and told me that he was sure that some of my nagging questions would be answered. We agreed to do a regression while we were both in Rhinebeck a few weeks later.

The night before, I lay awake for hours thinking about the regression, worrying whether I'd end up falling asleep again at the critical moment or if I would simply blank out. What if something had happened that I didn't want to know? My mind was spinning with all these questions, fears, and doubts, but above all, I desperately wanted it all to go well. I punched the pillow one more time in a vain attempt to get more comfortable, and told myself that everything that was about to happen would be what I needed — for my highest good. After all, I'd have Brian right there to assist and guide me. I totally trusted him.

The following morning dragged, and it seemed like ages before there was a gentle tap at my door. Brian met me at my room at our designated time. He calmly told me what to expect and how to prepare myself for my journey into my past lives.

"If you're ready, John, I think we should begin," he said.

I felt completely comfortable as he took me into a hypnotic induction that made me feel calm and quite safe. I relaxed as every part of my body began to unwind; and the nerves, tension, and worries just evaporated. My body somehow even felt lighter.

He started off by regressing me to an enjoyable childhood memory, leaving it up to my soul to go where that happy memory wanted to take me. As I drifted further, I could feel myself slipping deeper and deeper into relaxation. There was no conscious thought on my part of where I wanted to go. I just let it happen. I suddenly found myself at the beach with three friends. The clarity of that image was extraordinary.

"Where are you, John?" Brian asked quietly.

"The beach. We come here so rarely, but I love coming here," I replied. This was truly a happy memory, for when I was a child, going to the beach was a novelty, since we didn't live within walking distance of the coast. Usually in those hot and humid New England summers, we were the little hellions who were to be found opening up the nearest fire hydrant as we dared each other to stand under the freezing cold spray, which towered into the air. Of course, it always ended up with the fire department showing up and shutting it off. We'd be sent home with some stiff words, or threats to report us to our parents, as if that really deterred us!

In that state of total relaxation with Brian, this childhood memory had come flooding back (excuse the pun). I was aware that very moment that I was nine years old and could see and feel everything quite clearly on that beach. I experienced the smell of the salt in the air, the clear turquoise sky, the sun upon my face; I heard the rhythm of the waves rolling in and felt the coolness of the sand as I dug my feet deep into the wet seashore. It was as though I were actually there, and at that very moment, as far as I was concerned, I was. I could remember everything, from what I was wearing to the faces of my friends, even what we were talking about as we enjoyed that wonderful day on the beach. Without a doubt, this was definitely a happy memory for me.

Those of you who've read my first book will understand when I say that this was a memory I cherish because of my turbulent childhood. Of course, it's good to be reminded that there were those occasional enjoyable and happy times. It's easy to forget the good times when they were overshadowed by so many bad times. And it's so easy for the joyous ones to slip from our memory.

It was now time for me to leave this memory, as Brian slowly took me back even further to my mother's womb. This time I didn't fall asleep or drift off into oblivion. I was right there, in the moment, and fully conscious as if I were experiencing it all over again. I couldn't believe it. Yes, I was actually in my mother's womb!

"John, can you describe what you're experiencing right now, please?" he said. I remember telling him how calm I was as I floated inside my mother's womb.

"It's unbelievably quiet, totally peaceful, and so tranquil," I whispered as I looked around me. I could even see my umbilical cord pumping blood and nutrients into my tiny body. At that very moment, I felt my mother's love being projected to me through her thoughts and feelings. I also noticed something very unexpected, which was a soft bluish light that just seemed to surround me.

I knew intuitively that it wasn't a physical light, but a spiritual light. The light was somehow part of me, and I realized that I was witnessing the beautiful emanations that were part of my aura. This clear, pure, bluish glow somehow was protecting me as it wrapped strands of light around my tiny frame. I was awestruck when I noticed this, deeply moved; and even though I was under hypnosis, I could feel a tear run down my face on my physical body lying there on the bed.

Brian was still guiding me by constantly asking questions about what I was seeing and experiencing. He repeatedly reassured me that it was safe, as he sat right beside me. Somehow, he seemed close and far away at the same time. This experience in my mother's womb just reinforced what I've known my whole life: that we're not just physical beings, but are spiritual beings made of energy, love, and light.

It was now time to go back even further. Once again, Brian left it up to me to go back to a time that was important to me. I could hear as he counted down, and I drifted calmly and easily to another lifetime. Just as before, I couldn't believe the clarity that I was experiencing, and for a split second my rational mind crept in, asking: *Is this real? Am I imagining all this?*

Just as I was thinking that, Brian spoke up and said, "John, even if you feel it's your imagination, just go with it. Don't fight it." Either he's so experienced that he knows to say this to clients at this precise time, or he was aware of what I was thinking and feeling. I believe he was tapping into my experience and my soul. I let go and almost immediately noticed I was an old man, and just felt that I was somewhere in Wyoming. Even though I've never set foot in Wyoming, I just knew I was there.

It was really strange, if not a little unsettling for a second. I was this old man, but at the same time I was witnessing this strange scene, it seemed, from afar. I didn't feel the same sense of connection that I had with the memory on the beach, as though this was much farther back in my timeline. I could tell that I was in some type of wood cabin or shack, and realized that it was sometime in the late 1800s. I don't know how I knew what period I was in; it was more that I sensed it. The detail was extraordinary, as I could see the dirt floor, the walls, the windows, and the rain dripping through a hole in the roof. As if that wasn't enough, I could smell the heavy, musty air in the cabin; it was a strange odor. This place was falling to pieces, and I could clearly see I lived a life of poverty.

I was an old man, a priest or minister, and I was quite sickly and on my deathbed. I was dying from a lung disease; and in this life, amazingly enough, I find it's no coincidence that I was born with bronchitis. I had trouble breathing and became aware of my ever-diligent 14-year-old daughter, who was kneeling beside me. She was quietly placing wet rags over my forehead as she looked lovingly into my eyes. She knew I didn't have much time left on this earth. I was so worried she'd be alone, as my wife (her mother) had passed away years earlier. Tears welled up inside me, as the bond between us was so strong. I could feel the love and prayers coming from her. Right then, it dawned on me that my daughter in that lifetime is actually my mother in *this* lifetime! I just recognized her soul. Looking back, I don't know how I knew, but on the soul level — I simply did.

My mom and I in this lifetime have a special relationship. Yes, I'm her son, but I'm one of five children, and my mom has often told me that our relationship has always felt different. As a child, I was "the grown-up kid," the one who constantly worried about my mother, as well as my other siblings (if my dad was drinking). Even to this day, my brothers and sisters look to me as the head of the family. I'm the one they come to for major decisions about the well-being of my mom. Nothing ever gets done without my nod of approval.

Earlier I talked about how we switch roles when we reincarnate here. Well, I feel that my mom and I have exchanged different roles in many lifetimes. She may be my mother this time around, but we act more like friends. I've called her by her first name instead of "Mom" since I was a young child.

Back to that cabin. As the scene still played, I was now alone. The cabin was dark, and I could smell the damp emanating from the walls. I saw and felt myself slowly passing away, my soul leaving my body. I was able to look down at that body that no longer seemed to be mine. Who was that sick old man? I realized that although it belonged to me, I was no longer emotionally attached to that body or anything else — I was free. No more pain, no more sorrow, no more laboring to take my next breath. I find it ironic that in this lifetime, as I mentioned, I was born with bronchitis. Was it just a coincidence or what? I don't think so.

Many people who have phobias, unexplained pains or aches, or even birthmarks have interesting experiences when regressed. They usually go back to a lifetime that deals with an injury or a fear. Once they realize it's from another life, the pain or phobia usually leaves them. They realize it was a "carryover" from another life, and the attachment is often permanently severed.

As I floated above my own body with Brian sitting calmly beside me, he guided me to the "in-between place," a realm that is neither in this lifetime nor one from the past. It is a world of spirit and energy; and what took me by complete surprise, is that it is a world of the most beautiful and vibrant colors I've ever seen. It's almost impossible to put it down in words, as none can really capture what I was feeling or seeing, because when I think of it, how can I find meaningful and appropriate words to describe something that's spiritual and in this case nonphysical? One thing I can describe was the feeling of total peace that comes over you when you're no longer attached to a body or a life.

I was totally conscious, and my awareness was somehow enhanced as I knew immediately that I was no longer "John" but the *real me,* just pure consciousness. As I floated, it was totally amazing, as I was able to look down and watch all the different lifetimes that I'd experienced as a man, a woman, and even as a child. I could see how they all connected to the people and relationships in my present life to form this complex matrix. I knew that these lives spanned hundreds and hundreds of years, which provided me with another validation that the soul is eternal and never ends or dies.

I could see that there was a theme linking these lifetimes. I was, in fact, living a life of service as a holy or religious man in many of them. I could tell that I was a minister, rabbi, teacher, or even monk — many of whom had finely tuned intuitive psychic abilities. Therefore, I think it's fitting that in this life, I'm a medium and a spiritual teacher. I believe that at times we come back to do what we hadn't finished in a previous lifetime. Equally, we may stick to a theme that I believe we choose before we incarnate again.

We all have guides and helpers assisting us in our lives. Just as we have friends and people here who help us, so do we in the Spirit World. I've always known that I have my own guides and helpers, which became more evident while I was studying and developing my own mediumship. Every guide has his or her own "job" to do with us, whether it's protecting and educating, or inspiring and assisting us in this lifetime. Some stay with us forever, while some move on as we develop spiritually. I felt my own guides there in this in-between place. I saw their silhouettes, just off to the side, watching and somehow waiting to come forth. I noticed that I couldn't see their faces, but just felt their energy, presence, power, and more important — their unending love.

I could feel them drawing closer, as it was now time for them to communicate with me, their presence growing ever stronger. They didn't physically speak, but I could tell their thoughts were registering in my mind. It was like a two-way telepathic conversation. With their feelings and thoughts they projected enormous amounts of information, which registered into my consciousness and my memory. It felt a bit like a road map of what still lay ahead for me, along with some specific instructions about how I needed to take better care of myself. Sometimes, it's only when you get a message like this that it truly resonates, as they used words that they knew would strike a chord, for they referred to my body as my "vessel." Their message was clear: if I'm to continue doing this work, then I have to have my body, mind, and spirit healthy to sustain the level and intensity of the work that still lies ahead for me on this journey.

As I felt their energy stepping back, they wanted to leave me with a gift. They showed me souls coming over into the Spirit World. It's a scene I'll never, ever forget; for one day, I know I'll be one of those souls coming home again. I became aware of a bright light off to my left side, but the brilliance of this light didn't affect my eyes at all as I took in its wondrous radiance. I asked myself if this was actually God. To this day, I'm not sure, but I do know one thing: I felt a Supreme Intelligence and an overwhelming sense of pure love emanating from this light. There appeared to be many souls gravitating toward it. They were more like smaller sparks of light rather than physical bodies. I knew they were part of the bigger light, which became even brighter as each little spark blended with it. It was breathtaking, truly beautiful, and I've often wondered if any artist could ever capture what I was witnessing and do it full justice. If I can't find words to describe what I witnessed, I guess no picture would ever suffice.

There were other lifetimes that I regressed to during that session, but recounting them would take a whole book. I could hear Brian's voice in the distance calling me back, telling me that I would retain all the information that I'd seen, heard, and felt during my regression. I was slowly being drawn back to my own body, once again becoming aware of it and my immediate surroundings in this lifetime. How strange it felt to go from being completely free, experiencing my own soul and the Spirit World, to coming back into the dense molecular energy of my physical form and the earth. Brian and I had a few more words together about what I'd just experienced, and he quietly slipped out and left me there to be at peace and to think about the experience.

I realized after our session together that I might never work through or achieve all my plans or lessons in this lifetime, but it did make me even more aware of my role now in being an active participant in my life, enabling the continuing journey and growth of my own soul. I am truly thankful to Dr. Brian Weiss for allowing me to experience where I've been, the lessons I've learned, and the love I was fortunate enough to share and receive; but above all to understand even more who I am now, and most important, where I'm going.

# CHAPTER 12

## ANIMALS — OUR
## SPIRITUAL COMPANIONS

The power of an animal's love, intuition, and wisdom is greatly underestimated — whether it's an ape that not only understands but also responds to sign language, or a special cat that made the news by instinctively knowing when its nursing-home residents were about to leave this world. This particular cat would curl up beside those men and women to offer healing love and comfort. Then there's the dog that helps its therapist owner detect abnormalities in her patients' bodies, and the story of the amazingly brave elephants that impulsively knew they had to save themselves by moving to higher ground in the devastating tsunami that occurred early in the morning of December 26, 2004, off the west coast of Sumatra. Animals of all types are extraordinary creatures and are miraculous gifts to us.

Animals have been our spiritual companions since the dawn of time. Humans have honored them throughout history, as can be seen in those early drawings on the walls of caves — man and dog hunting side by side. Egyptians treated cats like gods, American Indians have honored many different animals on totem poles, and the elders in the tribes would teach the children about the importance and qualities of each living thing. It's my belief that animals have been placed on this earth to assist us in getting to know who we really are: namely, Divine sentient beings from God.

Long before I got my little dog Koda, a friend gave me a simple refrigerator magnet with a quote attributed to Anatole France. It speaks volumes to me: "Until one has loved an animal, a part of one's soul remains unawakened." Never have truer words been said. Animals help us let go, forget about the past, and remember that each day is a new opportunity. Whether they have fins, feathers, or fur, two legs or four — they touch our lives as well as our hearts and souls. They love us unconditionally and teach us to play, but most important, show us how to live in the now.

Animals are such healing creatures. Amazingly, dogs can detect when seizures are about to occur in their owners, and studies show that animals help lower our blood pressure, increase longevity after a heart attack, and even detect cancer!

I have a profound and deep connection with all kinds of animals that stems right from my early childhood. I never doubted their intelligence, intuition, wisdom, or their unconditional love. Living in the crammed conditions of a suburb of Boston, apartments were so tightly packed together that open space was scarce and hard to find. As a result, there wasn't much room for animals, so sadly, we never had a dog or a cat. Of course, pigeons were plentiful, and if I was lucky, a squirrel would make it through to the neighborhood and make its home in one of the few trees in the area. I was acutely aware of how much I longed for a pet of my own, even at that early age.

I was, as I have said many times, the "different" one in my family. I was psychically sensitive, socially awkward, and more often than not, I'd spend hours on my own reading instead of playing with my brothers and friends. It didn't end there, as to make matters worse I was skinny, wore glasses, had big ears, and inherited the nickname "Dumbo"! I know that doesn't paint a very attractive picture, but looking back, it wasn't a childhood I'd wish upon anyone today. In spite of it all I felt safe when I was with animals and nature.

There was many a time during those long, hot summers when an elderly neighbor, who was a bit like my surrogate grandmother, would take me into Boston to ride the Swan Boats. They were swan-shaped paddle boats moored in the small lagoon in the Public Garden in Boston. It was one of the popular pastimes for residents, and the tradition dates back to the late 1870s. Today, it's one of Boston's top tourist attractions! Yet for me, it was more about feeding the ducks and watching the real swans, as well as being in this huge open space. Even as a child, I would take it all in, absorbing the wondrous fragrances of all the flowers that covered the Public Garden. It had an amazing healing effect on me. For those few short hours, I could be myself, safe in the knowledge that I was, in fact, connected to all things.

Even the ocean called to me, but sadly, as I said previously, visits to the beach were few and far between. However, on those rare occasions when my brothers and sisters and I got the chance to play ball on the warm sand, I would wander off, spending time in quiet reflection in my own little world. I was fascinated by the power and magic of the ocean, and the many creatures that lived underneath the surface or farther out to sea in its deep waters. It's no wonder that as a young man, given the first opportunity, I became a certified scuba diver. My relationships with animals were often far easier than the ones I had with people. After all, there's far less drama in the animal kingdom; whereas *we* seem to create drama, and then some!

I get hundred of e-mails that touch my heart, especially those about animals, and when I combine my own experiences, it just proves the strength of the bond they have with us here and now and continue to have with us when they leave this physical world.

I remember one beautiful story that totally blew me away, even though it dates back to the mid-19th century. It's a tale about "Greyfriars Bobby," and this touching true story is a wonderful example of the love, loyalty, and devotion a dog can have for its owner.

Bobby was a Skye terrier that belonged to a police officer named John Gray in Edinburgh, Scotland, in the 1850s. Back then, police officers were required to have watchdogs as they made their rounds, and a terrier seemed like a perfect fit because they're known for their watchful eyes and booming voices.

Every day, Bobby would obediently follow his master on his daily rounds; wherever Constable Gray was, there was Bobby faithfully standing or walking right beside him. The two were pretty much inseparable until sadly one day in 1858, Constable Gray died of tuberculosis. The poor dog must have been incredibly confused, finding himself all alone as he sat beside his master's coffin. When it was time for the funeral procession, it's reported that witnesses saw Bobby walking proudly in line, constantly looking up at the coffin that was being carried by Gray's fellow officers.

Constable Gray was laid to rest in Greyfriars Churchyard. Later that day, the grave was filled in and friends, family members, and colleagues returned to their normal lives. You might think that as time went by, his grave would be forgotten, but in this case, there was his faithful and loyal companion Bobby. People would often see Bobby lying on his master's grave day after day, rain or shine, and began to feed him, until 1867, when it was decided that the ownerless dog should be put down. In a wonderful act of compassion, the Lord Provost of Edinburgh, Sir William Chambers (who loved and devoted much of his time to the prevention of cruelty to animals) paid to renew Bobby's license, which made him the responsibility of the town council.

In the end, Bobby amazingly kept his graveside vigil for his beloved owner for a total of 14 years, until he eventually died himself in 1872. Bobby was duly buried near Greyfriars Churchyard, and a statue of him was erected to honor his loyalty. I've told this story many times onstage, and I can easily see how it touches all who hear it. The bond between Constable Gray and Bobby has been written about in books and movies, and Bobby even has his own dedicated Website!

When we open ourselves to animals, no matter what kind, their souls truly touch ours. When animals communicate with us, it's done in a language where words are not needed. They speak the language of the soul, which in their case is love. I actually believe we learn more from them than they do from us. They are our spiritual teachers. They show us how to love, and more important, how to *accept* love. Animals push us beyond our comfort zones and show us how to reach out to others.

It's only when you have an animal of your own that this really starts to take shape. If it were not for my dog Koda, a little white terrier with a larger-than-life personality, I would never have met so many neighbors who have pets. As I write this book, Koda has just turned two years old, and I've been living in the same house for more than seven years. Until he came into my life, I never really met or realized that there were so many like-minded people who lived practically in my own backyard! Most of the people I've met are dog owners themselves, and somehow these creatures have bonded us, and now we share a special friendship.

As many readers probably have a pet or two, you'll know all too well that having one is in fact a partnership that works both ways. I truly believe that when you love and take care of an animal, you're somehow taking care of yourself in the process.

Of course, they're not just here for us, but just as much for themselves. Like us, they, too, have a journey of lessons and reasons for being. I'm still learning from Koda, as well as all the animals on the planet. We should honor them on all levels — physically, mentally, emotionally, and spiritually.

Animals help us to be so much more than we really are. They allow us to reach higher than we have ever reached before, to spiritual heights that we could never have imagined. All we need to do is . . . let them.

### *Animal Communication*

We may be uniquely distinctive and individual souls, but there's a commonality that binds us all together — a spiritual force. The same energy that makes up the stars in the sky, the same energy that courses through the Universe, is in each and every one of us . . . and that includes animals. As sentient beings, we're all connected. Animals have a way of knowing if we're sad, happy, tense, frustrated, or even sick. Many times we may not be feeling well; and as a result, our pets won't leave our sides. Animals simply know. They'll intuitively read our energy and act according to whatever they're *receiving* as well as *perceiving*. They have so much they want to teach and tell us, but for us, it's more a case that we just need to listen.

In my lectures, I'm often asked, "How do you begin to communicate with an animal or your pet?" Since animals can't speak to us in human language, and we cannot speak theirs, communication has to be done telepathically. For thousands of years, humans have used telepathy to communicate. It's quite common for a mother to feel that her son or daughter isn't well and to call that child, only to find out that there *is* something wrong. A wife and husband may continually finish each other's sentences or know what their partner is thinking. Suddenly you think about someone whom you haven't heard from for ages. The phone rings, and sure enough, it's the person you were just thinking about. These are just a few of the more common examples of what's known as telepathy.

Telapathy is the psychic communication directly from one person's mind to another without speaking, putting pen to paper, or any other signs or symbols. Since we're all connected by the universal power of energy and love, it's feasible that we should be able to communicate with our animal friends. From what I've experienced, animals are masters at telepathic communication and have an amazing ability to communicate with each other, as well as with us. Too many people think that animals are inferior to us, and that they lack the emotional and spiritual capacity that we possess. As a medium, and of course as a pet owner, I know for a fact that this is not true. Sometimes, as much as it pains me to say this, I've seen an animal act more compassionately than some humans do!

Even though I've been working as a psychic medium for many years, I never had the pleasure of meeting an animal communicator until recently. To be honest, I wasn't totally sure how I felt about it. Yes, I know you're probably saying, "But look what you do for a living!" Of course, I know animals can pick up and read our energy, but the question I asked myself was this: *Is it really possible to have a two-way communication with them?* Even if I did have some lingering doubts, I was about to get my answer.

Almost two years ago, I had just gotten back from an event and found myself sitting alone. It hadn't been that long since my partner of some 13 years and I had broken up, and feeling somewhat lonely,

I decided it was time to welcome a dog back into my life. I sat there going over the pros and cons, back and forth. I questioned if I had the time; that is, whether at this point in my busy life I had the dedication and patience to commit to a puppy.

I'd had a dog 15 years previously. Molly was a West Highland white terrier, but due to a rather bad breakup in an earlier relationship, I didn't get to take her with me, even though I had raised her, trained her, and groomed her. I remember the day I actually moved out, when it was time to say good-bye. I felt as though my heart was being ripped out as I took her in my arms one more time. I held her close to my heart as I cried, and sent as much love as I could to her. She was only two, and I guess I was sending her as much love as I possibly could since I knew I wouldn't be around anymore, and I knew she'd wonder where I'd gone.

Anybody who knows me or has read my Website or seen me onstage will know that one of my favorite sayings is: "Everything happens for a reason." Most of the time I'd say it makes sense, but at other times, such as this, I struggled to agree with it. With tears streaming down my face, it definitely didn't make sense to me to be leaving my dog, even though I knew she'd be in good hands.

It's strange how things happen, though. To this day, when I think back, I realize that had I gotten to keep Molly, I would have been tied to Los Angeles. I wouldn't have had the freedom to be able to go to England and study, and most important, to develop my mediumship. I probably wouldn't be where I am today! Had I stayed, I would never have met so many amazing people or visited all the countries I did. But as I left that day with the few meager belongings I possessed, I turned and looked back and saw her little white face peering through the window, paws pressed against the glass, looking at me with those sad eyes, as she always did every time I left the house. That was the last time I ever saw her.

I feel that when the time is right, an animal will often come into your life, and for all you know, it will have chosen you. In my heart, I knew I wanted another Westie, but I didn't really know where to start looking. They're not as common as Labradors, golden retrievers, or German shepherds. As I sat there, into my head popped that saying: "All thought creates reality." Impulsively, I made the decision. I didn't know at that moment, however, quite how soon the connection was going to occur.

The next day, I took advantage of a long-standing invitation to visit a friend and decided to drive down along the coastal route, as it is such a stunning drive. It was a beautiful sunny day, and I could see the sky and feel the ocean breezes, something that relaxes and inspires me. As I was driving, I noticed a woman walking her West Highland white terrier on the sidewalk. Something told me to stop, so I immediately pulled over, and she and I had a great talk about dogs. It was obvious how much she enjoyed her four-legged little friend, and she told me where the breeder lived. That afternoon, I called up, and lo and behold, she had a litter of puppies, so I arranged to go and see them.

Two days later, I drove over to see the three puppies — two boys and a girl. For a few seconds, memories of my last dog flooded back. At just five weeks old, they were scrambling on the floor, playing. I got down on my knees, and one little rambunctious male puppy walked right up to me and placed his head against my leg. He looked up at me, and we looked into each other's eyes (gulp), and I knew he was the one! Or was it the other way around, and it was in fact him saying, "Yup, this one's mine"?

He was ten weeks old when I got him. When I picked him up, I knew I was about to change his life, and somehow, I also knew he was about to change mine forever. I named him Koda, which in the Sioux Indian language means "friend." He looked just like a stuffed animal that you might find curled up on any child's bed or held under his arm as he enjoyed sweet dreams. Koda was cute as could be with his white coat, small black nose, and little pink ears. Although he was beautiful, he was quite a handful, but I don't regret one single day of having him. He has brought more joy, playfulness, and love into my life than I could have ever imagined. Over time, we bonded and connected on every level. That bond is probably stronger than some human relationships, as this little guy — as my mom calls him — is totally dependent on me taking care of his health, feeding him, exercising him, and washing him.

There have been times when I wondered if he actually knew what I was thinking, as he would tilt that little head at me and stare.

One spring evening in April, I was doing one of my many lectures at my favorite metaphysical bookstore, Circles of Wisdom, in Andover, Massachusetts. Before I went on, I was glancing through their catalog on the counter and noticed that an animal communicator was going to be speaking there. With Koda being such a big part of my life now, I inquired who she was and how she worked.

Danielle MacKinnon is an animal communicator in New England and is well known in her field. Many have testified that she helped them communicate with their cats, dogs, birds, horses, lizards, and even a mouse! To my surprise, many of my friends who have pets, and even my veterinarian, have had positive experiences with animal communicators. I knew that this was the chance for Koda and me to have the same experience, and I was certainly curious. I really wanted to meet Danielle to see if animals and humans can communicate with each other through the power of thought. What she told me still blows me away!

I called Danielle to make an appointment for Koda and me. Although she does many readings over the phone, I wanted to see and experience this with my own eyes. We were to meet two weeks later at Circles of Wisdom. I arrived with Koda in tow with a mix of excitement, curiosity, and intrigue about just how this was going to work. Danielle was quietly sitting there waiting for us. She's a young, attractive woman, with the friendliest, kindest face and a smile that could melt your heart. My psychic antenna was working, too, as I could feel the compassion she has for animals. It was really strong in her aura.

As soon as Koda met her, all you could see was a speeding white ball of fluff, as he showered her with affection and wet doggy kisses. I behaved more like a human and introduced myself with a handshake. She told me to simply let go of the leash and let Koda roam around the room. I was full of questions, but before I got a chance to speak, she pretty much stole my thunder by answering many of them as though she already knew. She told me all about herself, the extraordinary practice of animal communication, and how she works with all different types of animals. I found out that she works with both domestic and wild animals, and those that are ill, as well as all the healthy and happy ones. Naturally, as a medium, I was thrilled when I heard that she also works with animals that have passed. I felt an immediate bond with her. Clients ask for this service all the time, as it allows for grieving pet owners to feel a sense of closure about the loss of their pet; or in other situations, they're able to gain a deeper understanding of it.

She went on to explain that people come to see her for many different reasons. "John, just like you, many people come purely out of curiosity." She stopped to take a sip of water. "While there are times when I help people determine whether an animal is the right one for them, or whether their pet is adjusting to life with them as an owner, there are also those times when I become aware that an animal is ready to pass on."

Danielle told me how some animals open up immediately when the psychic connection takes place, while others take a little longer to warm up. "John, what's so amazing doing this work is how some pets start out slowly by giving playful, joking, or shy answers. Maybe they're just not sure what's happening, which is quite probable! However, once the trust between us is established and they understand what's going on, the animal will often communicate more openly."

She could see that I was looking at Koda while she was talking, who was sitting on the floor staring at me. His little dark eyes were looking at me, his master, with trust and love. I was putty in his little paws! She saw the strength of our bond and went on. "The depth of the connection with an animal depends on the animal's personality and can become even deeper when I earn their complete trust."

I'd come to this meeting with as open a mind as possible, but I really hadn't appreciated just how much animals psychically tell Danielle about their thoughts, feelings, emotions, the state of their body (health problems, emotional and environmental issues), and so much more. She told me how so many of her clients are surprised when their pets highlight their own personal issues. Clients are astonished by the number of things in their own lives that are mirrored by their pets — everything from low self-esteem to physical problems, and even changes in mood. Danielle explained how she works with the animal and the human to develop alternative behavior patterns. With cooperation from the human (owner), positive results can be achieved.

I'd already asked her if she was okay with my taking some notes for this book as she began our session. It was time, and almost as though he knew something was about to change, Koda sat up more alertly. Danielle started by acknowledging how much energy he had and how much he already cared for me. I was mesmerized as she directed her questions to Koda by telepathy, asking him whether he wanted to tell us anything. "John, Koda's telling me that his stomach has been bothering him." She turned to me and asked me whether he gets carsick.

"Not carsick, Danielle, but he was diagnosed with a parasite that he caught from a doggie day-care center that I've used a bit. I had quite a scare some weeks back when he got really sick, and I thought I was going to lose him." My voice trembled a bit as I told her this. "The parasite was infecting his whole digestive system, and he was quite sick for a while."

Danielle continued by asking, "So why is he throwing up little black things?"

Now this really blew me away. Little did she know that when I used to take Koda to puppy playgroup (as he just loved being with other dogs), the whole yard was covered with Astroturf, which is a form of fake grass. To prevent it from retaining water, the bottom of the turf is lined with minuscule black rubber pellets. Like all the puppies, Koda would play with the puppy toys. The tiny black pellets got stuck to the toys, and of course, he would ingest many of them unknowingly. There's no way Danielle could have known this, since only my veterinarian and I knew. With his digestive tract being weak from the parasite and the black pellets, his stomach was probably inflamed and sore. I explained to Danielle what the "black things" were.

"John, he's telling me that you take him to two other playgroups, is that right?" She went on and described the places, and I sat there listening as she even told me which one he preferred. Wow, I had no idea that he had opinions like this, and I thought, *This is totally surreal, she <u>really</u> is communicating with my little guy here!*

The reading went on too long to report everything, but she covered his eating habits; his sleeping area, which is right outside my bedroom; and how he loves to jump up onto the one particular windowsill and stare out into the woods. One more thing really sealed the deal! I could actually *feel* the exchange of thoughts between them. I was aware of every time she asked him a question, as he would stop playing and turn back to look into her eyes. I swear he was smiling!

She paused and turned around to look at me, "Is there someone else who often takes care of Koda?"

"Yes, there's a friend of mine who's been helping me since he was ten weeks old. When I travel, she comes to live in my home and takes care of Koda," I explained.

What happened next was truly amazing. Danielle started talking and acting just like this woman. She has a larger-than-life, colorful personality, and certainly has a highly expressive way of talking. I swear that Danielle took on the mannerisms and characteristics of this friend. I would have never believed it. It was a near-perfect imitation! How could she have picked up someone's personality in such detail unless Koda was sending her his impressions?

As the session ended, I was able to ask Koda some final questions through her, and then it was over. I was so impressed with Danielle, and although this was my first experience with an animal communicator, somehow I knew it would not be the last. The whole encounter solidified my belief that we're all connected, and that the power of love and thought can transcend how we communicate with each other.

Danielle finished up by giving me a few tips on how we can communicate with our pets, and she said that I could share them with my readers in this book. If you're seeking this type of communication, then I'd certainly suggest that you start off by seeking out a reputable animal communicator. Word of mouth is best, and even some vets use them, but trust your gut. With a bit of luck, you and your pet will have an amazing experience, which will strengthen the bond even more than you could ever imagine!

Here are some of Danielle's tips:

---

1. If you want to communicate with your pet, always ask for its permission first. Equally, don't forget to *thank* the animal at the end of the session.

2. When asking your pet a question, try to keep it short and simple. For example: "How are you feeling?" "What's bothering you?" "Do you like this?" Be as clear and concise as you can — that way, it will understand.

3. Animals like to think in pictures. If you're going out for a while, then imagine sending a picture of a clock to your animal with the time that you're expecting to return. If you're going away for a few days, then imagine how many sunsets you'll be away for. This is a new way of thinking, but once you get used to it, it will quickly become second nature, and part of your mind-set.

4. Try using your own body as a guide to connect with the body of your animal. Ask your pet if it's feeling all right, or if it's experiencing any discomfort, then see if you're feeling drawn to a certain area in your own body.

5. When animals communicate psychically with us through words, they most often speak only one word or in very short sentences. If you're looking to "hear" your pet psychically, don't be disappointed if you only receive "belly," "ear," or even "love walks." After all, this is how they really talk!

6. Animals also communicate with us in feelings. If you walk into a room and you're feeling sad for no reason, it could be your pet sending you that thought. Don't automatically disregard these feelings, but stop and acknowledge them, and see if you can feel where they're coming from.

7. If you're communicating with your pet and you start feeling yourself getting upset for the pet, your communication isn't going to be very clear, because *you're* not clear. If this happens, it's better to get yourself back to a state of being clear and balanced, then go back and try again. It's hard to be psychic when you're emotionally involved.

8. When you're talking about your pet to someone else, whether it's in the same room or you're miles away from it, always talk in a positive way about your animal, and never negatively. Since we're all connected, they're quite likely to tune in to your thoughts, the ones you think to yourself or the ones you share with others. Distance doesn't matter.

9. Be careful of your energy and moods. Animals are like one big psychic antenna. If you come home feeling stressed and you immediately start training your dog, then your pet will pick up those emotions and will act on what you're sending out. Try to remain calm and relaxed when you're with your animal. You'll get the same reaction back. When you want your pet to do something, picture it in your mind first and then project that image. You may be quite surprised when it does exactly what you just envisioned. Keep at it and practice, as eventually communication will strengthen both ways.

10. One last important tip Danielle gave me: Many animals tell her that they enjoy being animals and don't want to be treated as humans. Too many of us think they are humans in furry or fluffy coats, so once again, please respect their wishes and let them enjoy being animals.

---

If you already have a pet or you're thinking of getting one, then you might want to consider taking a class, whether online or in person, with an animal communicator. You never know, you might be better at it than you think, and it can only establish a stronger bond between you and the animal. After all, those little creatures have definitely come into your life for a reason. Usually, it's to teach unconditional love and to be teachers and healers as we all take our journey here together.

### *The Rainbow Bridge — Animals and the Afterlife*

One warm summer evening, I was walking Koda on the beach. It's a place where I can take him off his leash after 6 P.M. I swear it's one of his favorite times! He loves being able to charge across the sand, stopping to sniff every little bit of seaweed, or just chase the waves in and out as they come crashing on the shore. For me, it's such a special time — it's *our* time. I love watching him as he plays with the other dogs; and I know for a fact just how much he loves it, as I've now become aware when he turns around with a big thankful smile.

This particular evening, I noticed a woman sitting quietly in the sand dunes at the top of the beach, watching the beautiful sunset. Being the friendliest dog on the beach, of course Koda has to say hello to almost everyone and ran over to her. As I walked up to retrieve him, I could see her petting him fondly. Dogs are a wonderful conduit for allowing you to talk to anyone, and she said, "I had a dog many years ago. I'd love to have another dog, but I'm not sure that I could go through the pain of losing one again!" I know that the loss of a beloved pet can be devastating, and many owners feel they can never get another pet again.

Koda seemed determined to give her a little more attention, so I sat down for a few minutes to chat. "I truly understand, but you're missing out on *so* much joy and happiness now. Trust me, this little man has become such a big part of my life, and he shows me an unbelievable amount of love. You could have this in your life, too." I hoped that my words might bring some of the happy memories of her and her dog to the surface, since she seemed locked in her loss. I glanced over and noticed a tear trickle down her face as she remembered. I think it was more a tear of happiness than sadness, and as she got up to say good-bye, she turned back and mouthed two simple words to me: "Thank you."

I haven't seen her since on the beach, and who knows, fate could have put us on that dune at the same time that summer's evening for that brief encounter. Maybe, that's all she needed — to open up her heart again and create the space for a new pet.

If my experience with my dog is anything to go by, the bond that we have with our pets is very intimate. The connection is strong. Sometimes it can even be stronger than the ones we have with other people. Animals have a wonderful capacity to teach us to live life to the fullest, to make every day count; and most important, to be in the here and now. They are truly remarkable, as I believe they have a unique gift — to teach us about dying and death. Animals don't seem to fear death like we do. I believe they know they're going to a better place, they're going home; and I also believe that if we've forged a strong bond with our pets, they'll be there for us when it's our time.

I certainly don't underestimate that the death of a pet can be emotionally overwhelming. Their passing is often as painful for us as when we lose human loved ones. For some, when the relationship has been almost exclusively between them and their pet, the pain of loss can be even worse. People who don't own an animal may have a hard time understanding what pet owners are going through. The bereavement is real and profound. If you know people who have lost animals, please don't say something like, "But, it was *only* a dog," or "It was *only* a cat." All too often, people also make the mistake of then quickly saying, "So are you getting another one?"

No matter what kind of animal it was, honor the owners by allowing them to mourn and express themselves. Let them bring up the happy memories of their pets. It makes them feel good, and it's a far healthier way of dealing with the loss than locking the pain away. It can be a big change in lifestyle not having the pets with them, and for some, it's a big adjustment. In the most severe instances, it's about how they need to go on living themselves without the companionship of their beloved pets.

Danielle MacKinnon said when she links with an animal that's passed, the animal often tells her that it doesn't want its owner to be sad. I think pets want to let us know they were here to help us live a joyful spiritual life. They want us to continue with our lives and to be happy once again.

As a medium, I know that animals do have souls, and they do cross over to the Other-Side. I may not be able to communicate with them in the same way Danielle does, but they do come through, usually with another loved one. This just goes to show that the animals are not alone. There's always someone there for them, to care for them, until it's your time to do the job once again.

I'm forever trying to push myself further and further with validations as a spirit whisperer, and I try not to say something as bland as, "You lost a dog," or "You lost a cat." After all, most of us have had that experience at some point in our lives. In my readings, I usually now get the actual breed of the dog, as well as the coloring; and most of the time, I know whether it was small or large. The same goes for cats, but it doesn't stop there. I've also had birds, rabbits, chinchillas, mice, hamsters, and even horses come through. I was giving a message to a woman one night when I saw a very large white python wrapped around her neck. She screamed out in shock when I described the snake. It turned out that she'd owned a white python and would drape it around the back of her neck and shoulders. I remember that night vividly!

At the end of my lectures and demonstrations, I often do book signings, as it's a great way of getting a few minutes of private time with some of the audience members. So many people come to my bigger demonstrations with the hope that they'll get a message, but I'm only able to give so many with the time and energy I have. I don't make the choice of who gets a message — they do! One such night, a married couple came up to my table as I was signing books. The wife looked into my eyes with such sadness. As I was signing their book, I became aware of the spirit of a large sandy-colored dog sitting right in front of them. In that fleeting moment, I couldn't tell the breed, but I just knew it was big!

As they were turning to leave, I said, "Your dog is here with you, and what a big dog!" The woman turned to her husband and just sobbed into his chest; and as he lovingly wrapped his arm around her, he said, "We didn't come here for a connection with a person, but in fact were hoping to get a validation from our 125-pound golden retriever!" In those last few moments of the evening, the dog had come through in his own way. He hadn't let his "people" down.

There's a spiritual intelligence to all animals, as they're made up of energy just as we are. Since Koda came into my life, my connection to animals on the Other-Side has become stronger and clearer. It's as if my dog has strengthened my link to them. Koda's brought me yet another gift that has helped me, as well as countless others.

+·❊·+

Recently, I had the wonderful opportunity to meet a very special person. Her name is Dr. Ann Redding, and she told me about her unexpected experience with the Other-Side. Ann had taught biology for 27 years in California and was a typical scientist in the way she thought. As a result, she had a hard time believing anything that could not be proven by fact and logic. She viewed paranormal events, mediumship, and out-of-body experiences as amusing occurrences or figments of the imagination. Many people in the scientific world work mainly with the more analytical left side of the brain. I totally understand this, for many of us are brought up to not trust our intuition but to rely more on logic. When we begin school, we pull away from the more creative right side of the brain and begin to utilize the more rational part. When this natural shift takes place, psychic experiences and intuition take more of a backseat.

Some people have no knowledge of the paranormal, and their only reference is movies and television. These have a tendency to overdramatize psychic phenomena; and sadly, people believe what they watch, no matter how misleading the entertainment might be.

One day, Ann's own spiritual experiences would rock her logical world. Dogs had been her stable companions throughout her life. She was going to find it hard to dismiss what was about to happen, and it would prompt her to look beyond the limits of "explainable" science.

It started when she had what she called "visitations" from two of her deceased dogs. I wish I could have seen her face when that happened. Many people have had these experiences with pets they've lost. After these visitations, she decided to honor beloved pets everywhere by compiling a collection of true stories from pet owners who'd experienced after-death contacts with their animals. Together with the help of Ann Campbell, Dr. Redding wrote the book *Tails from Beyond: True Stories of Our Immortal Pets*.

I wholeheartedly recommend this book for people who have lost their animal companions. The stories describe how owners have experienced different visitations from their pets, such as the woman who reached down, thinking she was petting her living dog, and discovered when she looked that there was nothing there . . . or was there? There's another beautiful story about a woman who sees her dog as a speeding orange blur whiz by at lightning speed, as he did in real life. Then there's the touching story about an owner whose picture of a beloved pet glows on its own. Many people also dream of their pets. These ADCs are real and shouldn't be ignored. Just remember that your pet loved you in this life, and your faithful companion will continue to love you in the next.

When my dog was a puppy, he would often play by jumping on his hind legs, as if he were playing with someone or another animal. Don't be surprised when you lose a pet if you see something out of the corner of your eye, if you feel the animal lying on your bed, or if you dream about it. It's saying the same things that people do when they cross over, namely: "I'm here and I love you."

To have your own ADC from your pets, you have to first *believe* that it's possible. It could be a dream, a fleeting vision, a kiss from them, or just a feeling that they're there with you.

When we're going through the process of bereavement, many of us try to explain this form of communication as our imagination playing tricks on us. Whether human or animal, the soul is eternal, and our loving companions are not separated from us by distance, time, or even death. It's okay to put out pictures of them, remember them, and allow them to be part of our ongoing life by recognizing and accepting the signs as legitimate validations. In my book *Power of the Soul*, I mention that we're *not* just bodies with souls — we're souls that come with bodies. Animals are just like us in that they're souls that inhabited temporary bodies. When they cross over, know that they were *not* taken from us — just appreciate all the time that they were *given* to us.

+✷+

# Rainbow Bridge

(Inspired by a Norse legend)

By the edge of a woods, at the foot of a hill,
Is a lush, green meadow where time stands still.
Where the friends of man and woman do run,
When their time on earth is over and done.
For here, between this world and the next,
Is a place where each beloved creature finds rest.
On this golden land, they wait and they play,
Till the Rainbow Bridge, they cross over one day.
No more do they suffer, in pain or in sadness,
For here they are whole, their lives filled with gladness.
Their limbs are restored, their health renewed,
Their bodies have healed, with strength imbued.
They romp through the grass, without even a care,
Until one day they start, and sniff at the air.
All ears prick forward, eyes dart front and back,
Then all of a sudden, one breaks from the pack.
For just at that instant, their eyes have met.
Together again, both person and pet.
So, they run to each other, these friends from long past,
The time of their parting is over at last.
The sadness they felt while they were apart,
Has turned into joy once more in each heart.
They embrace with a love that will last forever,
And then, side-by-side, they cross over together.

# CHAPTER 13

## PSYCHIC TIME MACHINE

I stood there for that split second, caught in the horrific memory as though I were actually there. It felt so real. "They're all trapped! The screams are deafening!" I yelled at the cameras. "It's the part that they can't get out that's getting to me!" Warm tears trickled down my face. I felt choked with emotion as the full enormity of what had taken place started to materialize. I could barely speak. Even the television crew gasped as they followed me through what felt to me like dirty corridors. We were filming in the building I'd been asked to investigate. What I'm about to describe is one of the most emotional cases I've ever undertaken using my specialized ability of *place memory*.

Place memory is the ability to pick up vibrations and detailed information — whether it's seen, felt, or heard — of a past event. The more traumatic the event, the stronger the impressions. The easiest way to describe it is as if someone took a snapshot in time and etched it in the atmosphere of the actual environment or the fabric of the building where the event took place. Over the years I've been called to many locations; some are steeped in history, some are joyous, while others are imprinted with memories of tragedy and sadness, which can be quite overwhelming and emotional for me.

Fortunately, the majority of people don't have such finely tuned psychic antennae to be able to tap into such memories. Otherwise, we'd all be walking around looking shocked and miserable every time we go near a disaster site. On a lesser scale, many people may walk into a room and feel an argument that just took place or pick up on the atmosphere in a room that doesn't *feel* right. We've all experienced this sometime in our lives. In my case, I am able to go way beyond this feeling. My ability can be stretched over the canvas of time. It really doesn't matter if it was yesterday, last week, or even hundreds of years ago. Scenes play out in my mind as I slip back in time, and often the clarity and detail is like an old movie that's been digitally restored. I feel as if I'm actually there.

There are numerous subjective viewpoints on this subject, depending on your own beliefs. I believe that a haunting may not be a ghost, but it's one of these snapshots that plays continually, as though it's caught in a constant replay, imprinted into the fabric of time and space. People with highly tuned psychic antennae are more inclined to witness this phenomenon. As always, I never advocate that you take this lightly or think you can try it out. It takes years of study and guidance.

I became aware of this type of psychic work while training in the UK. A great teacher and friend, Margaret Stanley, was working with a Spiritualist church in the historic town of Devizes in the southwest of England. Many people flocked to this church, which dates back more than 800 years, due to its nontraditional teaching of psychic sciences and mediumship. Margaret wasn't afraid to try different ways and methods to educate her students and develop their often-dormant abilities. I quickly forged a good friendship with her, and became one of her regulars on her student psychic day trips. These were days when she'd take a small number of select students to some historical site or building. One of her top sites was the famous formation at Stonehenge. It's one of Britain's greatest national icons, symbolizing mystery and power. It's composed of earthworks surrounding a circular setting of large standing stones and sits at the center of the densest complex of Neolithic and Bronze Age monuments in England, including several hundred burial mounds.

Other times we'd find ourselves in a farmer's cornfield where a crop-circle formation had just been discovered, or we'd spend a day walking along the rugged cliffs admiring the dramatic landscape resulting from the long struggle between the land and sea. On still other occasions, we would visit the ancient castles and mansions of bygone days. These impressive buildings are all made of stone, and it seemed to me as though each stone could tell its own story. No matter what exciting place she arranged for us to visit, it was always a fascinating learning experience. I was in my element with all this history; and as I've written before, I felt completely comfortable, as though I'd been there many times in the past. With so much history and culture, it has to be every psychic's dream!

Margaret was a stickler about recording these experiences, and we never went out without our notebooks and journals. She encouraged us to go off by ourselves, walk the land, and record what we were sensing or feeling. I loved the days exploring those odd-shaped stone-walled rooms inside a historic castle or ruin. I recorded everything I picked up psychically in my journals. The beauty of those trips is that we never knew where we were going or were given any information. It was only at the end of the day that she'd explain where we'd been or the significance of the location.

Initially, I didn't tell Margaret that scenes would play out in my mind no matter where I visited, but as I became more confident and sure of what was happening, I opened up more. We'd all get together at the end of each visit, and Margaret, or sometimes a visiting historian, would provide further background information to validate our findings. This part was very important, as it gave me the absolute confidence to keep on with this work. I believe that that intensive year with Margaret, when I first realized I had the gift of place memory, was a critical part of my development. She was also quick to recognize it and encouraged me to develop it further.

I wonder now if Margaret knows what a profound effect she had all those years ago. How was I to know back then that television producers would utilize this rare gift in years to come? I wish all students of psychic sciences could have the opportunity to study with a mentor like Margaret. I'll always be thankful for her teaching, wisdom, and of course, her friendship. She remains close to my heart to this day.

### Triangle Shirtwaist Factory

I jumped as the phone rang. I'd been deep in thought, preparing for a demonstration later that evening, and picked up the receiver without really thinking.

"Hello, John, I'm a producer for a forthcoming TV special for A&E featuring five mediums. Would you be interested in being part of the show?"

The producer on the phone explained how she was searching the country for talented mediums to showcase their abilities. She told me that they'd already identified a medium to give a reading, and they had another medium lined up to investigate a haunted location. There would be a psychic detective who would actually be working on a current missing-persons case, and her fourth medium would be tested in a laboratory environment. With four mediums already identified, that left one more slot to fill.

"So we have all these mediums doing different things. What else could you do for the show?" she asked. At that precise moment, I felt all the memories of the UK and my experiences with Margaret flooding into my consciousness, especially my gift of place memory. I explained how it worked and how it could add a different dynamic to the program. I'd probably watched almost every show on TV about the paranormal, so I knew that something like this would be quite unusual. If it worked, it would be really dramatic. She immediately loved the idea and explained that it was up to her and the network to identify a suitable historic location for the filming. Before I hung up, I addressed the issue of skeptics, and explained that I should know absolutely nothing about where I was going. I even suggested that I should be blindfolded all the way to the location. From that moment on, I was kept in the dark. She dealt exclusively with my manager (who was sworn to silence) until the day I was collected to go to Logan Airport to fly to New York, destination unknown! I was on a late-afternoon flight, so I would be ready for an early-morning start the following day.

I sat on the plane feeling a bit like a coil of tightly woven wires, thoughts racing through my mind about what might lie before me.

I often find myself asking a barrage of questions, and this day was no different. Would I pick up something of the location, which I knew nothing about? How far back in time was I expected to go? Would the producer be happy? What kind of place were they taking me to? This was a whole new ball game compared to my usual routine of private clients, demonstrations, and workshops. This was going to be taped for TV, and I knew that I was going to be judged by millions, rather than the usual hundreds or thousands in a live audience.

As I sat there waiting for the plane to taxi down the runway, I could feel my nerves tightening around my chest, but at the same time, I was totally psyched up. Everything seemed to be happening slightly faster than normal. I had no say in where the producers were taking me. My manager had been true to his word, and all e-mails and logistics had been channeled through him. All I could do was trust that my guides would be there, and I knew I would give it my best effort.

The following morning, the producer and her staff met me in the hotel lobby with a blindfold. From this moment on, I was totally in their hands. People watched with interest as I was blind-folded and led out. I was plunged into darkness. Once in the car, I was informed that the cameras were rolling and were following my every move. New York in the summer can be very hot, and this was no exception. It was only 9 A.M., and already it was one of the hottest days in that summer of 2005, with the temperature set to rise into the low 90s. With the car windows open, I could smell the city and hear the traffic, as well as the buzz of people going about their day. It was a strange feeling, sitting there in the back of the car, slightly disoriented, but I knew it was time to open up my psychic centers — my chakras — in preparation to turn myself into a psychic time machine.

When you're blindfolded, it's strange how time can either race by or become indeterminable. In my case, I lost all track of time as though it almost stood still. It was about 30 minutes later that the car came to a stop. Nobody said anything as a production assistant took my arm and helped me out of the car. The producer checked one more time that the blindfold was quite secure. We really wanted to make sure there was no question about the integrity and validity of the filming.

They told me that we were about to go up in an elevator and that when we stepped out, we'd be at the location. Little did they know how disoriented I felt not being able to see in the car the whole way there, and that it had left me feeling a little nauseated. I couldn't wait to rip off that blindfold, not to just begin what I had to do, but to settle my stomach. As the elevator came to a stop, they escorted me out, and that's when they took off the blindfold. I had no idea what was going to hit me at that precise moment. This was one experience that for the rest of my life, I'll never forget.

For a few seconds, I struggled to adjust my eyes to the bright fluorescent lights of the space, as well as the camera crew with their lights. Still, hardly anything was said, apart from hushed whispers between the producer and crew discussing their equipment and angle shots. I was told I could begin. I looked around and could see that I was in a nondescript, lightly painted hallway. I paced up and down the long corridor a few times, aware of the cameras following my every move. I didn't feel as though I was getting anything until I came upon a closed door. It led to another hallway with stairs.

Before I opened the door, I turned around and told the producer, "I feel that whatever happened here has to do with women." It was hard to describe, but I just felt the energy of females, not just two or three, but lots of them. It was starting. I could feel myself slipping back in time, as I saw women with corsets, long skirts, and their hair tied up in tight buns. I knew enough about fashion to realize that I was somewhere around the early part of the 20th century. That's how I knew I was on track. The place-memory imprint was strong.

The producer signaled for me to continue as I made my way to the door, which led to the stairs down to the next floor. I opened the door and stood in the hall, and for a second was unable to move. I was hit by the overwhelming impression of people desperately trying to get down those stairs. I sensed their panic. It didn't make sense to me, as I felt as though they couldn't get out. This is the amazing part of doing this type of mediumship, because while I was linking with the past, my conscious logical mind in the present was thinking, *Where could I be?* My surroundings were just blank painted walls. *What the hell could have happened here?*

My body shuddered for a split second, and I let out an audible gasp. Suddenly, I knew that fire was involved. I could feel myself quickening again. "Is there another floor below me?" I asked, almost spitting the words out. Back onto the elevator we all went. The crew with all their cameras and lights managed to squeeze into the small elevator, which descended one floor. The elevator's doors opened, and I stepped out into a cavernous room. We must have been on the eighth or ninth floor now of the ten-story building. The whole room had been gutted, and there were a handful of construction workers putting up drywall. They were politely asked to leave us alone.

Soon the whole floor was empty and eerily quiet. All I could smell was fresh plaster and paint. I still had no idea where I was, and in a way, I was glad that the gutted room gave no evidence or clue. Just as I had done on the floor above, I began to see the fire in my mind and could hardly wait for the cameras to start rolling again. I waved them on and hurriedly said, "Let's go, let's go!"

I kept thinking and saying, "One big fireball, one big fireball! When this fire happened, I feel it was probably someone's stupidity, like a cigarette or something, and that this must have been big news in the day!" Now my psychic hearing was kicking in. I could hear machines in the background, creating a rhythmical *Ching! Ching! Ching!* They made a sort of roaring sound when all the machines were in unison. I could feel young women, younger than I was.

I was carrying on a constant dialogue with the cameras. I was totally amped at this point, walking back and forth. I don't think the production team knew what to do but to keep following me. I kept repeating the word "Textiles," while all the time I could hear the *ching, ching, ching* of machines! As I stood there, I could feel the sheer number of women who worked on this floor.

I kept thinking, *How could so many women have been packed in so tightly? What an awful working environment!* Even without the fire, how did they put up with such cramped conditions, coping with the heat of the machines in those hot summers before air-conditioning? It suddenly fit into place. I realized that what with the styles of dress, the cramped surroundings, the loud roaring of machines, and the rolls of fabric, I knew I was standing in a sewing sweatshop.

All my psychic senses were on sensory overload. I was *seeing* the flames, *feeling* the compact working environment, and *hearing* the loud roar of the machines. I could feel the conditions as my place memory kicked in further. I felt as though the production crew was far off in the distance. Every other conscious thought evaporated and left me experiencing that very moment. I have to state right here that I still had no idea where I was or any knowledge of the event that happened here. I hardly know New York City and had to take history in high school twice since I was so bad at that subject.

As I looked across the vast echoing space, it seemed strange that there were only two doors. I began to yell out to the production crew, "I want to go near those windows; I want to go over to that section of the room near the windows now!" I was being forcibly pulled toward them. The echoes of the past were reaching out to me with their long tendrils, holding me in their tight grasp. As I stood by the windows, the full horror and intensity of whatever had happened here dawned on me. I felt as though I was also living this nightmare myself. I felt the uncontrollable need to escape the fire that must have consumed many of these young girls' lives. Why was I being drawn to the windows and not the door? I was feeling the same exact things that these women must have felt. I could feel the terror running through their bodies, minds, and thoughts.

As I paced back and forth with the camera crew recording my every move, I made the sign to keep filming. I was holding back the tears and pain that I was experiencing. Then I could no longer contain myself as my emotions exploded, and I broke down and wept.

"It's the part where they can't get out that's getting to me!" My voice quivered, racked with the emotion of what I was feeling.

"Can't escape . . . can't escape . . . trapped . . . someone help us, the doors are locked, have to jump . . . have to jump!" I felt them screaming. It was deafening.

I heard the producer and the crew gasp as they witnessed me reliving this horrendous experience. What became even more apparent was that I could feel what these women were actually thinking just before they jumped. They were thinking of their lives, their families, their hopes and dreams, and of course, their fear. The fire was all-consuming, and they prayed it would end. Sixty-two of the women died when, realizing there was no other way to avoid the flames, they broke windows and jumped to the pavement eight floors below, much to the horror of the large crowd of bystanders who'd gathered on the street. The windows beckoned to them as they lined up one by one and hurled themselves out the window; some even jumped in pairs together to their death below.

There's also a story of a mysterious man whom people saw from the street below who seemed to be helping the women to the windows before they jumped. No one ever found out exactly who this man was. Was he simply someone who worked there, or was he a ghost or a spirit? I doubt we'll ever know.

In my mind, I was still trying to piece it all together. I couldn't stop thinking, *What happened here, and where am I? How could this disaster have happened? When will this experience end for me? I don't want to be here anymore — please make it stop!*

I could feel someone holding my arm as the producer tried to pull me back by slowly saying, "John, that's enough. Come back, relax, we have enough film now, you don't need to keep going." I could feel the tears running down my face, as I came back to the present. Suddenly I felt physically, mentally, and emotionally exhausted. There was nothing left for me to give, and I was relieved to break the link with that harrowing event. Looking around at the stunned faces of the film crew, I think they were equally drained. We knew going into this experiment with place memory that anything could happen. I think they got what they wanted and a lot more! As for me, I never thought I was going to relive such a heartbreaking story in such gory detail.

It was only after the program actually aired that I finally carried out more research. I found out that the company employed approximately 600 workers, mostly young immigrant women from

Germany, Italy, and Eastern Europe. Some of the women were as young as 12 or 13 and worked 14-hour shifts during a 60- to 72-hour workweek. Of course, the producers had hired their own historian to validate what happened during the filming.

## The Validation

As I sat down to take a moment to compose myself, and to wipe the tears and sweat away from my wet face, the producer introduced me to an historian who was an expert as well as being a tour guide for historical events and locations in New York City. She was a kind, soft-spoken woman and said she was amazed at the level of information and detail that I'd picked up, just from the fabric of the building. She told me the full story of what happened all those years ago.

The year was 1911, the late afternoon of March 25. A tragic fire broke out on the eighth floor of the Asch Building in the Triangle Shirtwaist Factory. There are numerous theories as to how it started, from a possible spark by a lit match or a cigarette to faulty electrical wiring. To this day, no one knows whether it was an accident or whether it had been started deliberately. Most of the workers alerted on the ninth and tenth floors were able to evacuate, either down the stairs or using the flimsy fire escape, which all too quickly buckled under the heat and became useless. Before long, the elevator also stopped working. Sadly, the warning about the fire did not reach the eighth floor in time, which only had two doors, one of which was locked, and the second stairwell was already full of smoke.

The historian told me that this was the most horrific event that had happened in New York City until the terrorist attacks on September 11, 2001. I made a mental note to myself at the time, thinking that the fire broke out in 1911 and the terrorist attack happened on 9/11. It's strange how the last three numbers of the year of the fire match the month and date of the terrorist attacks on the Twin Towers.

She told me additional stories of some of the women who worked there, mostly female immigrants under the age of 23. The working conditions were atrocious, with hundreds of woman lined up at sewing machines for barely $9 a week! These women were just happy they had jobs, and for many, it was the main income for their families. They all had hopes and dreams of making a life in America, the land of opportunity. Sadly, they never got that chance.

Although the building was considered fire-safe, it was probably a combination of the poor ventilation, locked doors, hazardous working conditions, and broken or missing fire escapes, which all contributed to the fire that swept through the clothing factory that afternoon in just 30 short minutes. It was ultimately responsible for the deaths of 148 workers, more than 60 of them jumping from the very windows that had consumed me with such emotion during the filming.

While the factory was supposed to be nonsmoking, I was upset to hear that one possible cause of the fire was attributed to someone smoking. It probably meant that a piece of hanging fabric had been ignited by a burning cigarette. As the historian told me this, I understood why I'd said earlier, "However this fire started, it was probably someone's sheer stupidity. The fire was the biggest news of the day!"

The historian continued her shocking story of the event and went on to tell me that when the fire broke out, the elevator was still working but the management had made sure their family members got out first. They'd left many people screaming for help.

Grieving relatives and hundreds of onlookers made their way to a temporary morgue at Pier 26 for the harrowing experience of trying to identify their family members as they looked over the bodies that lay in rows before them.

As I'm writing this, even though I filmed the special many years ago, I'm reliving the experience again. I had to walk away from my computer to take a break every so often and then come back to finish this chapter. The events of that day will stay with me for the rest of my life. The only comfort I receive is the knowledge that all those young women who perished on that tragic day are now safe, with their families on the Other-Side. It's also good to know that as a result of public outrage at the horror, numerous changes in factory and occupational-safety standards were put in place to ensure the safety of workers today.

I watched the TV special weeks later when it was finally edited. It's still a powerful and compelling piece of television. I was so glad that I had my friends around me when I saw it, for watching myself go through that experience was almost as if I were doing it all over again. I received a huge response from the viewing audience. Months later, the same production company asked me to go to another historical location blindfolded. Could I go through such a traumatic experience again? That story, I'm afraid, is for another book.

# CHAPTER 14

## FREQUENTLY ASKED QUESTIONS

It's often a sea of hands waving in the air that greets me when I open the floor for questions during any of my lectures and demonstrations. It's hard, when I'm staring out into the darkness, to figure out who's going to have that all-important burning question. Over the years, I've found it immensely rewarding to spend time answering as many questions as possible during these events. It's my way of giving back, of connecting on a one-to-one basis for a few minutes — my way of offering comfort and clarity. Equally, I try to answer as many e-mail questions as I can, so here are just a few of the more common ones, which relate to spirituality, mediumship, love, life, death, dreams, reincarnation, and so forth. Pretty much all my answers come from my own life experiences, as well as my own study and research. Therefore, as always, I just want to stress that the answers I provide are my *own* personal opinions and beliefs.

Some of the more frequently asked questions were featured in my first book, *Born Knowing,* and I've included them again in case you haven't read it yet. For those of you who have, I feel this information is well worth repeating. I sincerely hope that you'll find some answers you've been looking for about some of the pressing things you've been wondering about.

Probably one of the most frequently asked questions that comes up almost every time is:

**Q. Where is the Spirit World?**

A. A simple question, yet with such an important answer! Well, my belief is that it isn't above us or below us — it's actually all around us. I was taught to believe that everything is made up of energy and vibrations. The vibrations of this physical world where we exist in human form are slow and dense, whereas the Spirit World vibrates at a much higher rate. That's why it's invisible to the human eye. It's because it's vibrating at such a high frequency that we're unable to see it. Just like a dog whistle, we can't hear it due to the high pitch, yet a dog can. There's a thin layer between this world and the next (which I refer to either as "the Other-Side" or "the Spirit World"), and the only thing that separates us is the frequency of the vibrations.

So many people come to see me onstage and ask:

**Q. Can anyone become a medium?**

A. One of my favorite sayings that I learned in England is: "Mediums are born — not made." I really want to add that I firmly believe that *everyone* is born with a degree of psychic ability, and each and every one of us has the capability to improve and develop our awareness (psychically, intuitively, or on a deeper level of mediumship). We all have the ability to connect with our loved ones who have passed on through the power of thought and our dreams. Anyone who has seen me demonstrate will also know that another one of my favorite sayings, which has become part of my own brand, is: "Your loved ones are only a thought away."

We can assist them in contacting us by learning to increase and raise our energy — by doing so, we'll help in the communication by meeting them halfway.

So, to answer the question, no, I don't believe that *anyone* can become a medium. Rest assured, if you have the gift of mediumship, it's likely to present itself in its own way and in its own time. My last piece of advice with respect to this question is on a somber note. I do not recommend this as something that you should dabble with. It's such a serious subject and one that requires both delicacy and tact. It's not something that can be picked up and put down on a whim. If you find out that you do have the gift and want to eventually practice as a working medium, it will take dedication, patience, and time, as it can be a physically demanding job. Mediumship has to develop and grow; you'll find that most mediums spend their entire lives developing their abilities. One final point: you must also be ready to live a life of service.

Here's a question I always love to answer:

**Q. Are you open all the time to the Spirit World?**

A. Nowadays, my answer is firmly no, although it wasn't always quite as clear-cut. These days, when I go into a restaurant, I don't see all your friends and relatives joining you for dinner as though it's some huge family reunion! I've spent years training myself to shut off from those in the Spirit World when I'm not professionally working. *Why?* you may well ask. Simple: it's because I have a life here, and I need to be able to enjoy it without feeling as if I'm constantly on duty. In my workshops, I teach that we're spiritual beings as well as physical beings, and it's so important that we honor *all* of ourselves. It takes a really strong spirit to get my attention when I'm not working, as it needs to literally break through my shield, my "off switch," but on those rare occasions when one does, I've now learned that I still don't act on it every time. Just because spirits can come to me doesn't mean *they* are in control — I am. I wasn't so disciplined at the beginning, but then I was more inexperienced and possibly a little naïve.

As an example, I do remember one time when I was at a party where no one knew me. I was mingling with the guests when a young man walked in and pushed past me to get a drink. As he did so, I was aware that he'd lost a brother. I could *feel* his brother right beside him, right there at the party. I didn't really know quite what to do or how to behave. I had two choices, the first being to just blurt out something, and potentially shock this man by saying, "Hey, I know you lost a brother, and he's standing right beside you!" No, somehow I don't think that would have been the right approach. So what I did was this. I put my thoughts out to the brother and said, *If you want me to give your brother a message, then you figure out how that conversation is going to come about.* I put the responsibility on the spirit to work it out.

**Q. When it's my turn to cross over, will it matter what religion or faith I practiced?**

A. Most religions have some belief in the afterlife, some more than others. I do believe that it helps to follow some kind of faith, and through various teachings and a deeper understanding, that can assist us when it's our time to cross over. I often use the analogy of the spokes of a wheel, in that each spoke represents a different religion or faith, and although each is independent of the other, ultimately they're all moving in the same direction.

We're all born with the spark from the Divine (our spirit), so when our spirit crosses over, that spark will leave the "jacket" it's encased in and move back into the Spirit World where we all originated from. We all survive death no matter what (if any) religion we choose to believe in.

**Q. Are there different levels in the Spirit World?**

A. Most definitely. Every lesson and deed here determines what level you'll go to when you leave this physical world. You're incarnated into a physical body to assist you in your soul's growth, which is why it's so important to try to be the best you can be while you're here. You should continually strive to be compassionate and kind, and give assistance and love to others. This will always increase your rate of vibration. When it's your time to pass, your spirit will gravitate to its rightful level.

Now, here's an interesting question that pops up from time to time:

**Q. Are there bad spirits, and if so, do they come to you?**

A. In all the years I've done this work, I'm blessed to be able to say that I've yet to connect with a malevolent spirit or energy.

I have a strong code of ethics in the way I run my own life, so it goes without saying that I strongly believe in the saying "Like attracts like." I work for the highest good, consider myself a child of God, and believe in a Higher Power; therefore, I wouldn't attract this type of energy. I'm not that keen to call them "bad spirits," as I'd rather refer to them as spirits that exist at a lower vibration and dwell in the lower spheres of the Spirit World. They're just farther away from the Divine Source, so it will take longer for them to reach a higher level.

### Q. Are the spirits connected to us all the time?

A. Here in the physical world, your family and friends aren't around you 24/7, but when there's a crisis or emergency, they're there when you need them. Well, it's just the same way with your family and friends on the Other-Side. They often know what's going on in your life and try to let you know they are there for you, whether it's for love, guidance, hope, or even inspiration.

I'm convinced that few people actually realize just how much energy it takes for those who have passed to lower their vibration and make a connection to this physical plane. As a result, it's not something they're going to want to be doing all the time. I believe that they have their own learning to do over there and need time to grow and progress, which is why those who have recently passed often need time before they're ready to connect to the living.

### Q. Why do spirits come back?

A. It's simple — because they can! People on the Other-Side want to share our lives with us. Over the years I've been practicing as a medium, I must have done thousands of sittings where spirits have come through to acknowledge that they were around their loved ones during difficult times, and by doing so, they were able to lend their support and strength. Of course, they don't just visit when the going gets tough. By the same token, I often receive evidence that spirits were there to see their children get married, or witness the birth of a baby or a daughter's graduation. Holidays and special occasions are also big for them — they want to see us happy and like to take part in that joy. After all, if they were here physically, it goes without saying that they'd be present at these important events. Being in spirit doesn't change the fact that they're still our family and still care about us.

One of the big questions is always:

**Q. Do you call the dead to you?**

A. No, it really doesn't work like that. Just like us, spirits have free will — mediums don't have power over them. Most of the time, you'll hear from the ones you're hoping will come through with a message for you, but it's rare that a medium will guarantee who's going to come through. I've done many a reading with people who want to connect with a specific person, but end up hearing from someone they never expected. It isn't a case of 1-800-Dial-the-Dead!

Just such a situation happened recently when I sat with a client named Vivian who had great trouble walking, so I agreed to go to her home. I arrived, and she put me in her mother's room, sat me in her chair, and even made sure her mom's photos were all around me. Did she get her mother? You guessed it — no. However, a woman did come through for Vivian — a friend of hers. As I started to describe her to Vivian, she screamed, "What do *you* want?!" while looking up at the ceiling.

It turned out that ever since Vivian had lost her mom, she'd been a bit of a recluse. In the reading, her friend had come through to say that she was with her and wished she'd visit her other friends. I don't choose the spirits — they choose me and will often come through, not with the message you *want* to hear, but one you probably *need* to hear.

**Q. Can they help from the Other-Side?**

A. Just like those of us dwelling here, spirits can assist you, send you love and support, and even inspire you. However, it isn't their job to tell you what to do or to do it for you. *You* have to make your own decisions and take responsibility for your choices and actions. They can't interfere with the lessons you need to learn while you're here.

I remember a woman who was thrilled that her mother came through during our session. She wanted her mom to tell her if she should divorce her husband. Of course, the mother couldn't make that decision for her because it wasn't her job. The woman needed to take responsibility for her own life.

**Q. Can you give us your views on suicide?**

A. There's no point running away from your problems, as there's no real death, and sadly there's no escape from your dilemmas or issues. One way or another, you will have to deal with it here — or over there. Doing the work I do, I've linked with many people who have taken their own lives, and I always get a very different feeling when I'm communicating with them as opposed to a natural death. They're usually full of regret because they can see how those left behind are affected by their action. On the Other-Side, it's quite possible that they may be shown the difference they could have made in their own lives as well as the lives of others, had they chosen to stay.

When these spirits communicate with me, they rarely want to talk about how they passed, and they never link with me for very long. Usually someone who's passed before them, such as a family member or friend, will come forward to help with the communication. I believe that these spirits need all their energy to work on themselves, and they're going through a process of healing.

I always tell people that prayer can help those on the Other-Side who have taken their own lives, and in this way, they can be assisted in their healing.

One of the fascinating questions I'm asked is:

**Q. Do people change when they cross over?**

A. Each time I link with spirits, they usually appear to be exactly the same as when they were here. People seem to think that those who pass somehow turn into these exalted beings, yet they have the same personality and quirks on the Other-Side as they did before. They're still upbeat, humorous, strict, or relaxed over there. However, I do *believe* that spirits progress over time, raise themselves to a higher level, and evolve. Often they will impress me with their personalities or how they acted here so that the person receiving the message can understand who it is. It's a form of validation, which is a necessary part of the communication process. If someone was negative here, it's likely that they'll imprint that characteristic on me during the link, once again just to validate who they are. Have no fear. As souls, we all progress as we realize our faults, as well as whom we've hurt here, while we deal with all the decisions made in this lifetime. It's almost as if we have a *higher view* of things when we cross over and can see why certain things transpired.

It means a lot to my clients when I blend with the energy of their loved ones and start to describe and take on their personality or some of their individual habits. Since we're all so different, getting a spirit's personality can sometimes be the best evidence for a client.

**Q. Can you still communicate with my parents even if they didn't speak English?**

A. Yes, it's certainly possible. My type of mediumship works on a mental level, as I receive images and words through the power of thought, so there's no language barrier. I've read for Ethiopians, Chinese, Latinos, Brazilians, Japanese, and many more. Each time I connect with someone who has lived in another country, I always feel their culture, comprehend their language, and understand their experiences. In a funny sort of way, it's almost as if I'm actually there. Sometimes I may even come up with a word or saying in their language that I've never spoken before.

One time I did a reading for a woman who was from Romania. Her mom came through, and she'd never spoken English in her life. When she connected with me, it was all in pictures and symbols. I wasn't remotely surprised to find out that her mom was an artist and was a visual person. It was as if these pictures and symbols had words attached to them. In this case, the expression is true: "A picture is worth a thousand words." When a spirit wants to get a message across — trust me when I say that they'll do anything to make sure they get to do so!

**Q. What happens if one of my parents reincarnates before I go over to the Other-Side? Does that mean one or both won't be there when it's my time to pass?**

A. The best way I can describe this is an analogy that my colleague the medium Gordon Smith offered. Look at it this way. The soul is multidimensional. Imagine me as a computer, and with the computer is a hard drive, which is the oversoul. The oversoul is the bigger part of our soul. The program known as "John Holland" is currently playing, and when this program is finished (that is, when I pass away) the program will go back into the hard drive (oversoul), and another program from the hard drive will come forth and play out. So the program that is known as "John Holland," the personality and all the memories that I lived here in that lifetime, will always be in the oversoul. So have no fear, the loved ones you knew and loved here — will always be on the Other-Side waiting to greet you.

There are many levels to the soul, and as I've said many times before, the soul is multidimensional. All our lifetimes as a certain individual are stored in the oversoul, so a certain program should be fully accessible to a medium.

**Q. What do they do on the Other-Side?**

A. This is always such a great question! From the thousands of messages I've delivered throughout my career, some don't really say what they're doing, while others have no problem telling me what's going on with them on the Other-Side and what they do with their time. Basically, they can do whatever they wish. Some choose to enjoy what they did here in their earthly life. I had an elderly woman come through who wanted to tell her granddaughters that she was still gardening. I remember the look of sheer delight as they told me that she was a fantastic gardener and that working with the earth was her pride and joy. In another reading, this guy came through to tell me he was fishing, and in another message a group of young children who'd passed told me that they were still in some type of school. When some people pass over, they even go on to help those children who've recently passed adjust to being on the Other-Side. I'm always deeply moved by those stories. There are so many things they've told me they do on the Other-Side, but what I've noticed most is that what they were passionate about here seems to continue by choice in the Spirit World.

**Q. Does it matter how long people have been on the Other-Side before they come through?**

A. No, there is no set time limit. I've had spirit people come through many years after they've passed away — sometimes 30, 40, or even 50 years — or it could be as soon as one day. A friend of mine, Michael, passed away sadly due to complications from AIDS some years ago, and I remember being in his and his partner's home for the memorial service. His partner had spent some time setting up a room upstairs beautifully, with a handsome picture of Michael with some of the amazing artworks that he had drawn during his lifetime.

While I was saying my good-byes, I heard his voice speak softly in my ear: "John, please tell Amanda that I will do what I can from here to help her with money." I stopped for a second, in slight disbelief, thinking that it was strange, wondering whether it was just my imagination playing tricks on me or if it really was a message from him. I was still grieving his loss, since he had passed just two days before. After I had my own private conversation with him, remembering all the gallery visits and happy times we'd shared, and how I was blessed to have him as a friend in my life, it was time to say my good-byes, and I knew I would see him again.

I went downstairs, and of course, I just had to ask Amanda, "While you were upstairs, did you ask Michael something about money?" I knew it sounded very personal. She looked at me with a look of surprise and said as she put her head down, "Well . . . yes, John, I guess I was being selfish. I asked Michael if there was anything he could do to help me out financially over there; and if there was any guidance he could send me, it would be of great help now." I was amazed that he'd answered her so quickly.

So in answer to this popular question, no, it doesn't matter how long a person has been gone; it all depends on the people and how quickly they adjust to being in the Spirit World, and how fast they learn to work through a medium. They loved you here, they still love you there, and they want to help in any way they can.

**Q. If someone loses their spouse and meets someone else, is the one who passed away angry or upset?**

A. No. Most important, they want you to be happy. After all, you're the one who's still here and has to continue living in the physical world. When people come to see me for a private reading, having lost a spouse or a partner, it's clear that they find it really hard to move on due to their bereavement. Some people even feel guilty for being alive, and some who have met someone else feel as if they're cheating on their spouse or partner who passed away. Many times, those who loved you here and have passed away will orchestrate your meeting someone else. In a way, they become matchmakers in heaven!

So once again, it's our bereavement or guilt that prevents us from moving on. Rest assured, they're neither angry nor upset. It may just take a little time before you can even think about meeting someone else, and when you do, that person will never replace the one you loved before. It will be a new experience and a different kind of love, a love *they* want you to have.

**Q. If someone was married more than once — or had more than one love in life — whom do they end up with when they pass over?**

A. First, you have to realize that you're thinking in terms of physical love when you ask this question. Those on the Other-Side are no longer constrained by the physical body and its needs. If someone was married more than once or had numerous loves, they can gravitate to whomever they want, or go back and join the *soul group* from which they came. It's my belief that we reincarnate to this physical existence with the same people we've been with in numerous lifetimes, and that could encompass some of the loves and close relationships we've had here. I don't feel that we have just one soul mate, as many people in your life could be your soul mates. They could be your best friend, your partner, even someone whom you may have had a negative experience with. If there are those in your life who push you, challenge you, or make you reach far beyond your normal limitations, they're probably helping you advance as a soul — they could, in fact, be soul mates.

**Q. If there's someone you fought with, or whom you were angry with, and they passed away before you had the chance to forgive them for what happened, how do you deal with this?**

A. I get this question almost every time I do a lecture. Many people have had this happen to them. They might have been fighting with someone and said hurtful things to the person before he passed, or that person said hurtful things to them. These spirits always come through with forgiveness and ask for forgiveness themselves.

Believe me when I say that they know just by your thoughts that you've forgiven them and you love them. It's as though they have a higher view of things once they pass over and, as a result, they can see that they were in the wrong all along.

Have no fear that your loved ones care for you, and that they've let go of any resentment or anger. Love is eternal, and the love you have for them as well as the love they have for you is equally eternal. *That* is what they take with them.

**Q. If I have a sitting with a medium and no one comes through, does that mean that no one is there or they don't love me?**

A. Absolutely not! I've had sittings myself with other mediums, and some people whom I was close to here haven't come through for me. I believe they have their own lives over there, and often they're off doing their own thing. Maybe some choose to progress quickly and further, and while they will always love you, they're no longer attached to this plane of existence. You could be getting signs from them, and you may not even recognize the signs and signals they're sending.

In the Spirit World, they don't measure time as we do here, so they may still come through for you at a later date, or they may come through when you *really* need it.

One time I did a sitting for a woman, and no one came through at all. I told her that it didn't mean they didn't love her, and maybe it just wasn't the right time. We decided to try again in six months. When she came back, it transpired that in those months she'd lost someone quite close to her, and somehow those in the Spirit World held back in the last sitting because it was simply not the right time. This sitting was the one she really needed, with the most recent person coming through.

It may not always be the case, but give them a chance; let them know that you're open to a reading and that you're ready, because they take their cues from you. If they know that you're still very emotional, and you may not be ready for a reading and hearing from them, then they're more than likely going to hold back. No matter what the reason, remember they do in fact love you and will do anything they can to let you know it.

### Q. Are guides and angels the same thing?

A. My experience and personal belief is that a spirit guide has lived at some time or another on Earth in a physical body, while an angel has never had a physical incarnation. Every medium I know has one or more guides who work with them — some are constant, and some change during the medium's life, but each has their own unique influence over the development of the medium's gifts. As I've already mentioned, I have three of them.

Many ordinary people have these guides — it's not just limited to mediums. They may show themselves in many forms, such as a

Franciscan monk, an indigenous person, an ancient Egyptian, or even a child. I believe that they choose to show themselves in these familiar forms for our benefit. I feel that too many people place responsibility on these guides and expect them to do the person's work. Guides are here to assist us, not make decisions for us.

Angels are in a different category from guides — they're "messengers of God." Thousands of people from different cultures have had experiences with these beings. According to an ancient Jewish tradition, angels were the first intelligent beings, created by God to help sustain life and assist you in all areas of your life. Have you ever said to yourself, *How did I get out of that situation safely? It must have been luck.* Well, luck *may* have played a part in it, but it's more than likely that you had a little angelic assistance.

I remember being in a parking garage in Los Angeles once, and I was driving up a steep ramp. Another car came flying over that ramp in the opposite direction, coming right at me with lightning speed. All of a sudden, my car stalled right in its tracks. Had I continued to drive, I would have hit the approaching car head on, but because my car stopped so suddenly, the other vehicle had room to avoid me. Was it a random act of luck that my car stalled at that precise moment, or did I have a little Divine help? I think I know the answer to that one.

So, here's the final question that everyone wants to know:

**Q. How can I be more spiritual?**

A. In a way, I tend to answer this in all my books. It's one of my constant themes, and forms a major part of my teachings. Being spiritual is more than just taking a workshop or reading a book — *it's a state of mind and being.* How we live, what and how we think, how we love ourselves as well as others, and helping others in need is all part of being spiritual. We're always given the opportunity to raise our vibration to a higher level simply through our actions. So many people are trying to have spiritual experiences when the truth is simple: we're spiritual beings trying to have human experiences.

Acts of unconditional love and compassion are the highest forms of "being spiritual." Each and every one of us is capable of such wonderful and beautiful things. We can achieve so much with our time here, so let's embrace it!

❊

# EPILOGUE

## *Final Gifts*

As this book draws to a close, I want to say that I hope you've enjoyed sharing in my journey, in some of my amazing and heartfelt experiences, as well as some of the touching stories of some of the more memorable readings I've given as a spirit whisperer. As I've said repeatedly, I take my work seriously, and I plan to remain a student as I learn and grow in this life. As an observer, I'm constantly fascinated by, and grateful to, those on the Other-Side, as they continually reach out to guide and assist us here in so many ways. They're forever showing us that the Divine spark within us all keeps us eternally connected to each other.

I hope that reading my chronicles has not only demonstrated the power of Spirit, but helped you become more aware of the incredibly beautiful soul that you are. If this book has proven one thing, it's that love has no boundaries and continues beyond this physical realm, and that the *impossible* can indeed be *possible*.

I am comforted by the thought that in life, everything comes full circle. When I moved back to Massachusetts more than ten years ago as a relatively novice medium, I started off as a spirit whisperer giving demonstrations at a local metaphysical bookstore that only held 40 people, who would cram into this small loft space, sitting on colorful cushions. These evenings were intimate and provided a wonderful training ground for my mediumship. Once I conquered my initial fears, I quickly gained confidence and started to push myself as I learned how those on the Other-Side wanted to work with me. Little did I know that they were training me and preparing me to work with bigger audiences — step by step! Since then, I've demonstrated and lectured in front of thousands, and although I'll continue to do the larger events, I'll also continue with the smaller, more intimate gatherings, which are equally as exciting and rewarding.

One early summer afternoon last year, I was on my way to one of these smaller groups, which are called "The Gatherings." I'd turned off the freeway, and the pine trees stretched out for miles on either side of me. The sun was warming me, and with the sunroof half open, I felt invigorated, recharged, and inspired by nature after what had felt like a particularly long and cold winter. Then again, I probably say that every year!

As I'm driving to an event, I often find myself thinking about the group of people waiting for me. I know they'll be eagerly waiting to hear from that special someone. I'm aware of the expectations they have in coming to a demonstration, but I try to focus on the healing that I can bring for them. I let go of any doubts, and trust that even for those who don't receive a message, they'll still feel the benefit. There are those who will welcome any message, and sometimes there are a few people who are brought by a friend, and it's clear they simply don't believe! They say that seeing is believing, but sometimes *believing* has to come first, before anyone can witness the miracles that can happen right before us.

Someone once asked the great Scottish medium Albert Best if demonstrations of mediumship really convince audiences. He answered, "We can't convince anybody of anything. We can only sow a seed. The greatest thing we can do is to stimulate people to find out more for themselves. We can't take away the pain of loss, but if we have taken away the fear of death, if we have given hope where there was none before, then we have done something worthwhile." I feel that pretty much says it all.

I started this book writing about the connection between a mother and her child, how helping parents who've lost children has inspired me to continue to do this work, and living a life of service to Spirit and those here who need my help. So as I finish writing, I'd like to leave you with a story from that early summer afternoon. It illustrates that life is truly precious. Do all that you can now; live life to the fullest; strive to be more than you are; reach out to others who need your help; be grateful, and connect with those who are in your life now and tell them how much they mean to you, because you never know what tomorrow may bring.

As I parked my car that day, I could already feel the spirit people drawing close. The best way of describing it is like a shift, as though I have one foot in this world and one foot in the other. Every time I walk into an event, I usually find everyone sitting quietly, waiting, and most likely calling on their loved ones in their thoughts to please make their presence known. Today was no different.

I was about two hours into the demonstration, and time seemed to be speeding by as I moved from person to person, giving messages with specific validations. Mothers, fathers, grandparents, aunts and uncles, children, and friends had all come through. I was just about to finish, as I could feel the energy from the Other Side begin to fade, when I heard a voice that was directing me to an attractive couple right up front. I knew I had to give this one last message.

"I feel I want to come right here," I said, pointing to the front row. "The state of Florida is being highlighted in a big way. Do you understand that, please?"

"Yes, John," was the quick response of the gentleman.

"May I ask your name, sir?"

"My name is Brian, and this is my wife, Carol," he said quietly as he reached out for her hand, as if some force was giving them strength for what was about to happen.

"Which one of you lost your father, please?" I asked, although I already knew that Brian would raise his hand. "Brian, I know that Florida is a popular place to visit, but I feel it's more significant to your parents."

"Yes, John, my mom lives there, and we've just gotten back from visiting her."

"Well, Brian, your dad is coming through quite strongly," I went on. "But he's got someone with him who really wants to come through. Your dad has a younger energy with him." I paused for a second as I realized who was coming through. "Did you and Carol lose a child?"

Carol and Brian hardly missed a heartbeat as they both spoke, "Yes, John, we lost our son." The energy in the room was electric, with everyone offering their love and support to this couple.

At this point, the link was crystal clear and the information was coming in strong, so I gently went on. "I feel that he passed from an illness, and I can feel a slight pain behind my eye. Was he eight years old?"

Bryan looked directly into my eyes as though he were talking to his son again. It was clear that he was obviously reliving the day that his son was diagnosed as he went on. "Our son, Ryan, passed away from a brain tumor, and he'd just turned nine when he left us."

The whole group could feel the love for that boy, and everyone was being touched by this final message of the afternoon. I could feel the wave of compassion being sent to Ryan's parents.

"Brian, your son keeps saying to me, 'My daddy was holding me, and I died in his arms.'" Tears flowed down their faces, and I noticed many of the audience members wiping their tears away. I couldn't let myself get swept away by the same emotion and tried to hold myself together.

Carol later told me that Ryan was a happy little boy, even though he knew he was sick. He never, ever complained and continued to laugh and play like any normal child. I feel that it's the children who become the heroes when they have a life-threatening illness. Somehow, in some way, they seem to help us remain strong, as though they know they'll leave us. Well, that day did come on July 28, 1988. The same angels who brought him to his loving parents, Brian and Carol, were the same angels who took him home to heaven. He was not alone.

Suddenly, I could feel Ryan's grandfather right beside him, helping his little grandson continue with his heartfelt message to his parents. "He's so proud of you, Brian! He's letting me know that you're a police officer." That made Brian smile.

"Yes, John, I work in law enforcement!"

Ryan was telling me that his dad was more than a cop. "He's making me feel like you deserve stripes or something. Are you a captain?"

"Actually, John, I'm a detective," he said, knowing that his son had been fascinated by the stories he used to bring home.

I chuckled, as I was seeing a scene that was playing out right in front of me, compliments of Ryan! "Well, I don't believe what your kid is showing me. Now let me get this right, Brian: you're a detective, and you've *just* been pulled over by the police yourself!"

The whole audience burst out laughing through their tears, and Brian had no problem yelling out, "*Yes!* Last week! Oh my God!"

I wasted no time in responding to the amusing moment. "See, they know what we're up to more than you think. It's further proof that they're still part of our lives."

Ryan didn't want to forget his big sister, as he continued to wow me and his parents, as well as the rest of the small gathering. He clearly wanted me to go on. "You have one daughter, is that correct?"

"Yes, we have a daughter, Erica," Carol confirmed.

"Well, he's saying that he's an uncle now."

Brian and Carol were thrilled to hear their son acknowledge this. When a child is born into a family after the loss of another family member, such as Ryan, there's a sense of sadness in thinking they'll never get to know the newborn child. I went on to tell Ryan's parents and everyone else in the room, "Don't worry if a child is born after someone passes, because in reality, they met your child *first*. They usually meet in the Spirit World before the child is born here."

At this point I could feel that Ryan was really showing off.

"Please tell your daughter that he's aware that she had two more children."

"Yes, John, that's true."

Without even a pause, I blurted out, "Twins, right?"

"Yes!" they both exclaimed with looks of surprise on their faces.

"Hey! Your kid's good! Please tell your daughter he's watching over her and the whole family. He's happy and loves you all so very much. He's with his grandfather, and he didn't want this afternoon to end until he came through to let you know that."

I could feel Ryan and his grandfather stepping back. The cord was weakening, and then . . . I was alone. I was left with the feeling that of all the messages that came through that summer afternoon, one little boy touched the hearts and souls of *everyone* in that room. I really feel that the people who didn't get a message still took away something very special to share with others.

As everyone started to make their way out, I could see Brian and Carol walking up to me. Their faces glowed brighter than when they'd arrived. Brian shook my hand, and I gave him a big bear hug. Carol, with eyes still full of tears, put her arms around my neck and pulled me closer to her. She kissed me on the cheek and softly whispered in my ear, "God bless you, John. I waited 21 years for that message."

Brian and Carol took each other by the hand and slowly turned to walk away. I knew they were not walking out alone that day.

When I called Carol to ask her if it was okay for me to include Ryan's message in this book, she and Brian were both thrilled and told me that they'd shared their experience with so many people since then. She thanked me once again for being a conduit and said they were forever grateful. Finally, as we were saying good-bye, she said to me, "John, I now know that love goes on forever, and there are signs and wonders all around us." I think her words are a gentle reminder for everyone reading this book right now.

I feel that we can all learn from those wise words, and it proves to me once again that in a way, we are *all* spirit whisperers. All we have to do is simply . . . listen.

# RECOMMENDED READING AND RESOURCES

## Books

*All My Relations: Living with Animals as Teachers and Healers,* by Susan Chernack McElroy (New World, 2004)

*Angel Numbers,* by Doreen Virtue and Lynette Brown (Hay House, Inc., 2005)

*Animals and the Afterlife,* by Kim Sheridan (Hay House, Inc., 2006)

*Born Knowing,* by John Holland with Cindy Pearlman (Hay House, Inc., 2003)

*The Care and Feeding of Indigo Children,* by Doreen Virtue
(Hay House, Inc., 2001)

*Glynis Has Your Number,* by Glynis McCants (Hyperion, 2005)

*The Grief Recovery Handbook,* by John W. James and Russell Friedman
(Harper Perennial, 1998)

*Hello From Heaven!* by Bill Guggenheim and Judy Guggenheim (Bantam, 1996)

*The Highly Sensitive Child,* by Elaine N. Aron, Ph.D. (Broadway, 2002)

*The Indigo Children,* by Lee Carroll and Jan Tober (Hay House, Inc., 1999)

*The Intuitive Spark,* by Sonia Choquette (Hay House, Inc., 2007)

*Is Your Child Psychic?* by Alex Tanous and Katherine Fair Donnelly (iUniverse, 2000)

*Life Among the Dead,* by Lisa Williams (Simon Spotlight Entertainment, 2009)

*Living Images,* by Coral Polge and Kay Hunter (SAGB, 1997)

*Looking Beyond,* by James Van Praagh (Fireside, 2003)

*Many Lives, Many Masters,* by Brian Weiss, M.D. (Fireside, 1998)

*A Medium's Cookbook: Recipes for the Soul,* by Suzane Northrop (Northstar, 2005)

*Messages from Spirit,* by Colette Baron-Reid (Hay House, Inc., 2008)

*One Last Time,* by John Edward (Berkley Trade, 1999)

*Power of the Soul,* by John Holland (Hay House, Inc., 2007)

*The Power of Your Spirit,* by Stephen O'Brien (Voices, 2003)

*Principles of Spiritualism,* by Lyn G. de Swarte (Thorsons, 1999)

*Psychic Navigator,* by John Holland (Hay House, Inc., 2004)

*Soulful Parenting,* by Susan Gale and Peggy Day (A.R.E. Press, 2008)

*Tails from Beyond,* by Dr. Ann Redding and Ann Campbell (Outskirts Press, 2008)

*Transforming Fate into Destiny,* by Robert Ohotto (Hay House, Inc., 2008)

*Unfinished Business,* by James Van Praagh (Harper One, 2009)

*The Unmistakable Touch of Grace,* by Cheryl Richardson (Free Press, 2006)

*When a Pet Passes On,* by Alison Landis Stone (Healthy Pet Magazine/Douglas Drew Publisher, February 2008)

## Organizations

The following organizations are those I've worked with; and others that I admire, respect, and recommend:

**Al-Anon/Alateen**
(888) 4AL-ANON
www.al-anon.alateen.org

**ARE Association for Research and Enlightenment**
(757) 428-3588
www.edgarcayce.org

**Bella Spark Productions**
www.bellaspark.com

**Celebrate Your Life! conference**
Mishka Productions
(480) 970-8543
www.MishkaProductions.com

**Circles of Wisdom bookstore**
(978) 474-8010
www.CirclesofWisdom.com

**Danielle MacKinnon, animal services/animal intuitive**
www.daniellemackinnon.com

**Friends Communities**
www.friendscommunities.org

**Hay House Radio**
www.HayHouseRadio.com®

I Can Do It!® conference
Hay House, Inc.
www.icandoit.net

Image Shaper
www.ImageShaper.biz

Infinite Quest
www.InfiniteQuest.com

Infinity Foundation
http://infinityfoundation.org

Inspired Gatherings
www.inspiredgatherings.com

Journey Within
www.journeywithin.org

Lily Dale Assembly
www.lilydaleassembly.com

Ofspirit.com Weekly Magazine
(207) 967-9892
www.ofspirit.com

Omega Institute
(845) 266-4444
www.eomega.org

A Place of Light
(508) 892-8928
www.placeoflight.net/

Spirit of Change
www.spiritofchange.org

Transformations Holistic Learning Center
www.readytotransform.com

## Bereavement Information

**Bereaved Parents of the USA:** A nationwide organization designed to aid and support bereaved parents and their families struggling to overcome their grief after the passing of a child.
www.bereavedparentsusa.org

**The Compassionate Friends:** A nationwide organization of bereaved parents offering friendship, support groups, and one-on-one assistance in your area.
**www.compassionatefriends.org**

**Helpguide:** Understand, Prevent & *Resolve* Life's Challenges
**http://www.helpguide.org/mental/grief_loss.htm**

**Wings:** Information and inspiration for the bereaved and caregivers, including a quarterly magazine of real stories about people's journeys through grief.
**www.wingsgrief.org**

## *Life-After-Death Information*

**After-Death Communication (ADC):** A comprehensive site produced by Bill and Judy Guggenheim, the authors of *Hello From Heaven!*
**www.after-death.com**

## *UK Resources*

**Arthur Findlay College**
Stansted Hall
Stansted
CM24 8UD
UK
Phone: + 44 (0)127 981 3636
**www.arthurfindlaycollege.org**

**College of Psychic Studies**
16 Queensberry Place
London SW7 2EB
UK
**www.collegeofpsychicstudies.co.uk**

**Spiritualist Association of Great Britain (SAGB)**
33 Belgrave Square
London SW18QB
England
Phone: +44 (0) 207 235 3351
**www.spiritualistassociation.org.uk**

# ACKNOWLEDGMENTS

Every author understands the value of good support. I truly appreciate the special friends and colleagues who support me while I'm immersed in the process of writing a book. Over the years, I've learned to structure my life over the many months of writing, and even though writing can often be quite solitary, I'm blessed with a group of people in my life who have been there for me to listen, pull me up when I need it, support me, keep me grounded, and at times they're just there to tell me as it is! They help me through the many various stages of the creative process, and encourage and push me to be even more than I am . . . and above all, which is the best part, they respect and love me for just being me.

Let me first express my appreciation to: God, the Universe, Spirit, and my guides. The guidance and blessings given to me are my deepest treasures, and I hold them close to my heart and to my soul. I am eternally grateful.

To my family, especially you, *Jennie,* for your love and the laughter we share when we spend quality time, and for the many talks we share together. I love you, Ma!

A special "Thank you!" to my constant friend and business manager, Simon Steel, for his dedication and enduring patience over the past 14 years. He's a master at sculpting my words into works of art. He has his own unique gift of being able to see the big picture and has constantly held my best interests close to his own heart. D.Y.L.M.T.

To Pat and Ken Steel and the whole Steel family, I love you all. You'll *always* be my second family. To Victoria and the Griffin Angels, Jessica, Emily, Anna, I've watched you as babies grow into the beautiful young women you are today. I'm very proud of what you've all achieved.

To Meryl Goldsmith, thank you for coming into my life just at the right time — another wonderful example of synchronicity. By being part of my team, you're helping to heal and touch many lives.

To Debra Eriksen, for your friendship and support, you've been there in this life with me, and most likely we've connected in past lifetimes. I'm sure we'll find each other in future lifetimes as well. You've been an example to so many in the way you've handled your own losses this past year.

To Bob and Melissa, Cheryl, Michael, Kerri and Missy, Bruce, Max, Vincent, and Gretchen — thank you all for the learning, love, and laughter we have shared. I love you all.

Suzie and Damien, thank you for your friendship as well as your inspiration, and for being the best aunt and uncle to our boy. To Brian and Carol Weiss, don't ever change, you two! My soul sister Colette Baron-Reid and Marc, I treasure our times together and the learning and laughter that's so much a part of our friendship. Lisa Williams, Kev, and Charlie, what a breath of fresh air you all are! A pleasure meeting and knowing you; may we remain close for a very long time.

Inma, to you, a big thank-you! One little white puppy and the Universe brought us together just when we all needed each other. Elizabeth and Beanie, our walks together mean more to me than you'll ever know. Suzane Northrop, a colleague and more important a dedicated friend. To Liz Dawn and the whole family at Mishka Productions, and no forgetting Ariel, I know you're watching!

John Edward and the whole team at Infinite Quest. John Matson, for your tireless creative work on the *Psychic Tarot Deck;* together we created a piece of art and work that speaks for itself. To Circles of Wisdom in Andover, Massachusetts: Cathy Levine, Bob, Laura Wooster, Joy, and the whole staff, thank you for your continued support. You're my favorite metaphysical bookstore!

For all those who have shared their stories, by sharing and letting people into your lives, you'll create a ripple effect that will touch thousands of hearts. To my students, and most important, to you, the reader, who continue to be my ultimate teachers in this lifetime.

To all my teachers, colleagues, and friends in the UK: knowing all of you has brought me more than you could ever know.

I couldn't finish these acknowledgments without mentioning my beloved Koda. You may not be able to read this, but you've taught me to be present, to be myself, to laugh, and to play each and every day! To Diane: You gave me such a precious gift — which changed my life. Thank you.

To the Hay House family: Reid Tracy, thank you Sue H for your encouragement, advice, and wisdom! A special thank-you to Louise Hay for inspiring the world and me. Nancy Levin, I'm sure that you know how much so many of us appreciate and care about you.

A special thank-you to: Jill Kramer, Jessica Kelley, Margarete Nielsen, Bridget Broschart, Bryn Best, Charles McStravick, Nick Welch, Melissa Brinkerhoff, and Anna Almanza — I appreciate all your help (with everything)!

To Mollie, Adrian, Christa, Donna, Craig, Matt, Rocky, Chris, as well as all my fellow authors, I'm honored to be part of the extended family and to be involved in the purpose of enlightenment and positive change.

To the team running Hay House Radio: Summer McStravick, Diane Ray, Joe, Kyle, and Steve, thank you for your continued support putting *soul* into radio!

To Ron, George, Ibis, and Ericka at Life Journeys Travel, thank you so much for all your help and hard work on our *special* cruises. The oceans have never been the same!

And finally, to all the people I've been unable to mention, I'm truly blessed by simply knowing you all.

# ABOUT THE AUTHOR

**John Holland**, author of the bestseller *Born Knowing*, has become one of the top psychic mediums and spiritual teachers. He regularly lectures throughout the United States. His public demonstrations provide audiences with a rare glimpse into the fascinating subject of mediumship, which he delivers with his unique style, combining subtle humour with the capacity to link to the Other-Side with clarity and passion. John has spent a significant part of his life developing his abilities, and spent two intensive years studying in the UK, where he believes that he got the thorough grounding and training to become a professional medium of absolute integrity. As a result, he has devoted his life to service and to Spirit.

He has starred in several TV specials, including A&E's *Mediums: We See Dead People*, which provided a fascinating insight into how John works as a psychic time machine. He's able to pick up vibrations and detailed information, whether it's seen, felt or heard from a past event. He has also starred in his own pilot, *Psychic History* for the History Channel.

John can be heard every week as he hosts his own Internet radio show on Hay House Radio: *Spirit Connections*. He's dedicated to the ongoing development of his unique gift and brings real integrity to his profession.

John says, 'If I can help people connect with someone on the Other-Side; and bring peace, comfort, and perhaps some closure, then I've done my job.'

www.johnholland.com

To contact John:
P.O. Box 983
Exeter, NH 03833

Phone: (617) 747-4491
**www.JohnHolland.com**

# Hay House Titles of Related Interest

**YOU CAN HEAL YOUR LIFE**, *the movie,*
starring Louise L. Hay & Friends
(available as a 1-DVD program and an expanded 2-DVD set)
Watch the trailer at: **www.LouiseHayMovie.com**

**THE SHIFT,** *the movie,*
starring Dr. Wayne W. Dyer
(available as a 1-DVD program and an expanded 2-DVD set)
Watch the trailer at: **www.DyerMovie.com**

✦❖✦

**Angel Numbers 101:** *The Meaning of 111, 123, 444,
and Other Number Sequences,* by Doreen Virtue

**Animals and the Afterlife:** *True Stories of Our Best Friends'
Journey Beyond Death,* by Kim Sheridan

**Communication with All Life:** *Revelations of an
Animal Communicator,* by Joan Ranquet

**The Intuitive Spark:** *Bringing Intuition Home to Your Child,
Your Family, and You,* by Sonia Choquette

**Messages from Spirit:** *The Extraordinary Power of Oracles,
Omens, and Signs,* by Colette Baron-Reid

**The Times of Our Lives:** *Extraordinary True Stories of Synchronicity,
Destiny, Meaning, and Purpose,* by Louise L. Hay and friends

**Your Soul's Compass:** *What Is Spiritual Guidance?*
by Joan Borysenko, Ph.D.

All of the above are available at your local bookstore,
or may be ordered by contacting Hay House.

✦❖✦

# JOIN THE HAY HOUSE FAMILY

As the leading self-help, mind, body and spirit publisher in the UK, we'd like to welcome you to our family so that you can enjoy all the benefits our website has to offer.

 **EXTRACTS** from a selection of your favourite author titles

 **COMPETITIONS, PRIZES & SPECIAL OFFERS** Win extracts, money off, downloads and so much more

 **LISTEN** to a range of radio interviews and our latest audio publications

 **CELEBRATE YOUR BIRTHDAY** An inspiring gift will be sent your way

 **LATEST NEWS** Keep up with the latest news from and about our authors

 **ATTEND OUR AUTHOR EVENTS** Be the first to hear about our author events

 **iPHONE APPS** Download your favourite app for your iPhone

 **HAY HOUSE INFORMATION** Ask us anything, all enquiries answered

join us online at **www.hayhouse.co.uk**

 292B Kensal Road, London W10 5BE
T: 020 8962 1230 E: info@hayhouse.co.uk